*How to Tell if Your
Child Has a Drug/Alcohol
Problem & What to
Do about It*

DRUGS
& your kid

Peter D. Rogers, Ph.D.
Lea Goldstein, Ph.D.

New Harbinger Publications, Inc.

Publisher's Note

Distributed in the U.S.A. by Publishers Group West; in Canada by Raincoast Books; in Great Britain by Hi Marketing, Ltd.; in South Africa by Real Books, Ltd.; in Australia by Boobook; and in New Zealand by Tandem Press.

Copyright © 2002 by Peter D. Rogers and Lea Goldstein
New Harbinger Publications, Inc.
5674 Shattuck Avenue
Oakland, CA 94609

Cover design by Salmon Studios
Edited by Brady Kahn
Text design by Michele Waters

ISBN 1-57224-301-5 Paperback

New Harbinger Publications' Web site address: www.newharbinger.com

04   03   02

10   9   8   7   6   5   4   3   2   1

First printing

For Matt, whose love, support, and great hugs enrich my life.

—P.D.R.

To my mother Anne, my role model for great parenting.
And to my son Noah, for giving me the chance to pass on
her wisdom.

—L.G.

Contents

Foreword   vii

Introduction   1

CHAPTER 1
  Is My Teen Using Drugs/Alcohol?   3

CHAPTER 2
  Putting Drugs in Perspective   21

CHAPTER 3
  Designer, Rave, and Club Drugs   37

CHAPTER 4
  How Do Drugs Affect Teen and Family   51
  Development?

CHAPTER 5
  Why Is This Happening to Us?   65

CHAPTER 6

What Doesn't Work   81

CHAPTER 7

What Does Work   91

CHAPTER 8

What to Do If Your Teen Is Abusing Alcohol   113
or Drugs

CHAPTER 9

What to Do If Your Teen Won't Cooperate   127

CHAPTER 10

Hope   145

APPENDIX A

Street Slang   159

APPENDIX B

Resources   169

APPENDIX C

The Twelve Steps of Alcoholics Anonymous   173

References   175

Foreword

Drugs and Your Kid provides a valuable guide for families battling with the issue of substance abuse. I read this book from two perspectives: as a physician specializing in addiction medicine dealing with adolescent addiction issues for more than thirty years (since I started the Haight Ashbury Free Clinics in June of 1969), and as a parent who has a child with a substance abuse problem. Clearly, one looks at such a publication in a different way, depending on if you are a physician, a parent, or as in my case, both.

While looking at this book as a parent, chapter 1 is especially striking: Is My Teen Using Drugs/Alcohol? I have four children, three of whom are doing well, and one who is in the early recovery process from substance abuse. The Parent's Awareness Checklist is a clear and practical way to begin to discern whether a teenager is using drugs or alcohol. Many of the signs and symptoms on this checklist were right in front of our family's noses. And even though we are professionals, we either didn't or couldn't bear the idea that our child's dramatic change in direction was a result of substance abuse. Although all of the guidelines are valuable for parents (including those with expertise in chemical dependency, such as myself), the one that struck me was number seven: "My teen has dropped out of sports or other extracurricular activities." Parents may come up with all sorts of reasons why changes are happening, as I did. When I found out that our child's involvement in sports had substantially declined, I rationalized that our child was rebelling because of my own sports fanaticism (since our shared activity in the early years always revolved around playing and observing sports). The reader of this book will find many signs and symptoms that will apply. Accepting the evidence that's right in front of a parent's face is very painful, which is why the checklist is so valuable—it objectifies a highly subjective and emotional issue.

Although the drug reviews and the adolescent drug trends will be valuable for the parent who is unfamiliar with this information, I found the section on adolescent development especially relevant. Particularly useful was the description of the adolescent's unique set of developmental tasks, including: establishing a positive identity, separating from caregivers, and acquiring an education. Subsequent chapters dealing with codependency and communication styles that don't work are invaluable, especially once parents understand their child's developmental tasks. For example, separation from caregivers, particularly in a family such as ours, in which both parents are in recovery, is a very difficult one.

Various other components of the book—such as measuring success and preventing relapse—will also be helpful, as the authors stress the need for seeking professional help, particularly as a consequence of breaking family rules. These guidelines will be essential for any parent, whether trying to prevent substance abuse in their children or dealing with substance abuse that has already occurred within the family. This book contains important information whether or not a parent has knowledge of addiction or is in recovery. As both a parent and physician, I understand that parenting in this complicated, high-risk world is a very difficult task, and *Drugs and Your Kid* provides a valuable guide in dealing with this challenging and emotional issue.

—David E. Smith, MD
Founder and President, Haight Ashbury Free Clinics, Inc.
Adjunct Professor, UCSF
Medical Director, California Alcohol and Drug Programs

Introduction

In the small universe of the chemical dependency community even parallel lines sometimes intersect. We had led parallel professional lives for many years, until our paths crossed at Kaiser Permanente hospital. There, Peter was the chief of the Chemical Dependency division, and Lea was director of the Adolescent Chemical Dependency Program.

Lea is a clinical psychologist who has worked with adolescents and their families for the past twenty years. She has worked in both inpatient and outpatient settings, as well as maintaining a private psychotherapy practice focusing on family therapy.

Peter is now retired, after spending more than thirty years as a clinical psychologist working primarily in the field of substance abuse. He is still administrative director of the Haight Ashbury Psychological Services clinic in San Francisco.

This book is the result of many hours of conversation between us, which began when we started working together more than five years ago. We quickly realized that we held congruent points of view about the nature of chemical dependency and its roots in adolescent development. We also realized that we wanted to have a positive impact on a wider audience of parents struggling with drinking/drug abusing teens. And so we began fantasizing about writing a book. What you're holding in your hands is our fantasy come true.

We believe that you, as parents, are the best prevention and treatment program for teen drinking and drug abuse. All you need to do is *look* at your teen's behavior, *listen* and understand what they're saying, and *respond* in a helpful way. This book provides you with the tools, information, and resources that can help you do just that. The most important thing is that you be willing to take an active, positive role in your teen's life. Your teen may not like some of the interventions that you choose. But please believe us, in the long run they'll thank you for saving their lives.

CHAPTER 1

Is My Teen Using Drugs/Alcohol?

Ashley, an only child, was her parents' pride and joy. Born loved and loving, she was a sunny child, the princess of the playground. When she grew to be a teenager, however, she turned inexplicably dark and sullen. She dyed her hair black, and painted her fingernails to match, listening only to morbid and dark music. Avoiding family and friends, she sought comfort in solitary pursuits. One day she passed out at school and was taken to the infirmary. The school nurse discovered tracks (needle marks and blackened collapsed veins) on her arms. What had happened? Was there any way to have prevented this from occurring?

This chapter is designed to help you understand and communicate with your teenage child. It encourages you to take a good hard look at what's going on in your child's world. No family is above or beyond the possibility of a drug problem. Just think of President George W. Bush's daughters' underage drinking and his niece being arrested for prescription drug abuse. Even Prince Charles's son Prince Harry has abused alcohol and marijuana. That's why it's so important to take the time and make the effort to really pay attention and look at your teen. Most parents usually have an intuitive feel if something is wrong, or if their child is trying to hide something. Pay attention to that feeling because you're probably on the right track.

How Can You Tell?

The following checklist covers behaviors common to most teenagers. Many of these behaviors are a normal part of growing up. That's why it's so difficult for parents to differentiate between a teen who's just going through a phase and one who has become dangerously involved with alcohol and/or drugs.

Go down the entire list and put a check mark by all the behaviors that pertain to your teen. We'll help you analyze the results when you're done.

Exercise: Parent's Awareness Checklist

☐ 1. I've been suspicious of my teen's general behavior, even though I can't quite put my finger on what's wrong.

☐ 2. My teen's grades at school have gotten suddenly worse.

☐ 3. It's become difficult to get my teen involved in family activities.

☐ 4. My teen has made a radical change in appearance or the clothes (s)he wears.

☐ 5. My teen stays out at night past curfew time.

☐ 6. I've noticed that my teen has started hanging out with a different crowd.

☐ 7. My teen has dropped out of sports or other extracurricular activities.

☐ 8. My teen has become secretive, hiding out in his/her room.

☐ 9. My teen has become increasingly isolated and is now a loner.

☐ 10. I've noticed that my teen seems to use excessive amounts of eyedrops or breath mints.

☐ 11. My teen has become uncooperative and more argumentative than usual.

☐ 12. My teen seems obsessed with music that involves drugs and violence (like gangsta rap).

☐ 13. My teen has been suspended from school or been ordered to attend detention classes.

☐ 14. I've noticed that my teen appears to be depressed or anxious.

☐ 15. I've noticed that my teen has become verbally or physically abusive to other family members.

☐ 16. I've noticed that my teen seems to be spending an unusual amount of time sleeping.

☐ 17. My teen has been cutting classes at school.

☐ 18. I've noticed that my teen sometimes laughs excessively for no apparent reason.

☐ 19. My teen has become rebellious and defiant.

☐ 20. My teen has been caught stealing from family or friends.

☐ 21. I've noticed that my teen seems withdrawn from the family.

☐ 22. My teen sometimes comes home drunk or smelling of alcohol.

☐ 23. I've noticed that my teen tries to avoid contact with us when (s)he comes home.

☐ 24. My teen has started to smoke.

☐ 25. My teen spends long periods of time in the bathroom.

☐ 26. My teen receives mysterious phone calls at all hours.

☐ 27. I've noticed that prescription medications have been disappearing from the medicine cabinet.

☐ 28. My teen has been expelled (or quit) school.

☐ 29. I've noticed that my teen's eyes are often bloodshot, or his/her pupils are dilated.

☐ 30. It seems that valuables have been disappearing from my house.

☐ 31. I have found suspicious items around the house and in my teen's room, and I think they might be drug paraphernalia.

☐ 32. My teen has openly admitted to using alcohol, marijuana, or other drugs.

☐ 33. I've noticed that my teen sometimes appears to have large amounts of cash.

☐ 34. My teen has been arrested for vandalism, shoplifting, and/or breaking and entering.

☐ 35. I've noticed wine bottles missing from my wine cellar.

☐ 36. My teen has been arrested due to an alcohol- (or drug-related) event.

☐ 37. I've noticed that my teen has persistent respiratory problems.

☐ 38. My teen has threatened (or attempted) suicide.

Now that you've finished checking the behaviors that relate to your teen, it's time to do the same for your own (and your spouse's) behavior. It's natural, as concerned parents, that some of the behaviors listed below will apply to you.

☐ 39. I spend a lot of time worrying about my teen's problems.

☐ 40. My spouse and I argue all the time about our teen's behavior and often disagree.

☐ 41. There have been times when I felt relieved when my teen leaves the house.

☐ 42. Sometimes I make excuses for my teen's behavior when talking to others.

☐ 43. I've tried to cover up some of the things my teen has done.

☐ 44. I sometimes give money to my teen without telling my spouse.

☐ 45. I have felt frustrated because nothing seems to make an impact on my teen's behavior, no matter what I do.

☐ 46. I believe that I'm a failure as a parent.

☐ 47. I've tried unsuccessfully to bargain with my teen in an attempt to change his/her behavior.

☐ 48. I often feel angry at my teen.

☐ 49. I feel sad because sometimes I don't like my child at all.

☐ 50. I'm concerned that my teen is becoming out of control.

☐ 51. I'm afraid that my teen might hurt himself/herself or others.

☐ 52. I feel very badly because I've had to compromise my own values concerning my teen's behavior.

Now go back over the checklist and tally up the number of items checked:

Group A   Items 1–12 _____

Group B   Items 13–26 _____

Group C   Items 27–38 _____

Group D   Items 39–52 _____

The behaviors in group A could indicate drug/alcohol-related problems. Hopefully, you've checked only a few items in group A and none in the other groups. If so, your teen's behavior most likely falls into the "normal" or experimentation range. Now may be a good opportunity to have a discussion with your teen about your concerns. It's also a good idea to start paying closer attention to your teen's behaviors and activities.

If you checked *all* the items in group A or several items in all four groups, we strongly recommend that you seek the help of a professional counselor.

The behaviors clustered in group B indicate misuse or possibly even abuse of drugs or alcohol. These behaviors also suggest that your teen is not doing well living in the world at large. It looks like your teen is having difficulties in managing his/her life successfully.

If you've checked several items in both group A and group B, we strongly suggest that you schedule your teen for a professional evaluation. This will help to determine if your teen is having psychological or drug/alcohol problems.

The behaviors clustered in group C are signs that your teen has either been abusing drugs or alcohol for some time or is developing serious psychological problems. They may also indicate that your teen is drug dependent or physiologically addicted.

If you've checked some of these items and several from groups A and B, it means that your teen is in urgent need of an evaluation and professional help.

The behaviors in group D represent the behavior of parents who love their teen and want desperately to believe that everything is okay, but sadly, it's not. If you've checked a number of items in this group, you might be caught up in the subtle behavioral traps of denial and enabling. What this means is that you could be ignoring or making excuses for the telltale signs of alcohol/drug use. You might unwittingly be creating an environment that actually rewards or reinforces your teen's inappropriate behavior. (We'll discuss this further in chapter 6.)

Current Drugs of Abuse

Today's teens are usually better informed about drugs than their parents are. The following information is to be considered a basic primer, not an exhaustive treatment on the subject. The information presented here is as accurate and up-to-date as possible.

Parents usually want to know the warning signs of drug abuse. So we've included behavioral indicators of drug/alcohol use and abuse wherever possible. Also, parents often ask what it feels like to be on these drugs, so that information has been included as well.

Our aim is to enable you to hold your own in a reasonable conversation with your teen. Please don't misuse this information in a well-intentioned but misguided effort to scare your kids. It won't work.

There are basically seven categories of drugs in common usage on the streets: cannabinoids, opiates, depressants, stimulants, psychedelics, inhalants, and the catch-all category—designer, rave, or club drugs. We'll cover the first six categories here. You can find out more about designer, rave, and club drugs in chapter 3. We've also provided a complete list of drug "slang" in appendix A.

Before we go on, it would probably be helpful to clarify the concept of addiction. Addiction is best defined as repetitive, compulsive use of a substance; a behavior that continues despite repeated negative consequences to the user.

When professionals use the terms physical addiction (or physical dependence), they have a specific set of criteria in mind. A substance is considered physically addicting if 1) over time, more and more of the substance is required to achieve the original effect (i.e., the user builds up tolerance) and 2) a rebound effect, commonly known as "withdrawal," occurs after drug use is discontinued.

The terms psychological addiction (or dependence) can be applied to drugs such as marijuana and LSD, which are not physically addictive.

Cannabinoids

Marijuana (also known as pot, grass, or weed) and hashish (a concentrated form made from the resin of the marijuana plant) are actually mild hallucinogens, but they deserve a section all to themselves. The active ingredient is THC (tetrahydrocannabinol). Marijuana is usually smoked in a pipe, rolled in cigarette papers as a joint, or packed in a cigar (blunt). Sometimes it is even baked into cookies or brownies and nicknamed Alice B. Toklas (a play on words, since "tokeless" means not having to inhale). There is *no* overdose potential and *no* physical addiction, although chronic users may develop a psychological dependence and build up tolerance to THC. Since THC is stored in the fatty tissues of the body, traces can be detected by drug tests for as long as six months to a year after the last use.

A study recently conducted by Connecticut's Marijuana Treatment Project Research Group confirms that long-term heavy cannabis users show impairment in memory that gets worse over time (Solowij et al. 2002). The study does not suggest in any way that pot causes serious brain damage.

What it feels like to be high on marijuana. In low doses, being stoned on marijuana is like getting a little tipsy on alcohol. You feel relaxed and have a tendency to giggle a lot. At slightly higher doses, time appears to slow down, and there can be a psychedelic effect, such as lights flickering. At really high doses, there is the danger of paranoia, thinking people are after you, and a tendency to withdraw into yourself.

Behavioral indicators. Eyes may become bloodshot, but your teen may use eyedrops. The odor of marijuana smoke, something like burnt rope, can be masked by the burning of incense. Cigarette rolling papers, pipes with wire-mesh inserts, or bongs (large glass pipes) lying around are a good sign that your teen smokes marijuana. Unusually high consumption rates of take-out pizza may suggest the munchies. There are no signs of psychological withdrawal, other than general restlessness or irritability. Long-term use may result in apathy or lack of motivation.

Opiates

Opiates are derivatives of the opium poppy. They are grown as a cash crop in many places in the world, including Afghanistan. All opiates are narcotics, which have a sedative effect and are generally strong analgesics, or painkillers. (In fact, they can actually increase the user's threshold for pain.) Heroin, a highly addictive opiate, is illegal in the United States. Other opiate derivatives that are prescribed medications, such as codeine or morphine, can be used illegally.

Heroin

When heroin (black tar, chiva, smack, or junk) is combined with water and cooked in a spoon, it becomes a liquid that may be injected into a vein or into a muscle. Persian heroin may be smoked by heating the chunks on a piece of tin foil and inhaling the smoke with a straw (known as "chasing the dragon"). Higher grade forms of heroin can be snorted like cocaine. This is done by "drawing lines" using a razor blade on a mirror, or other hard surface, to finely chop the drug and form short parallel lines. The drug is then rapidly inhaled, one nostril at a time, using a straw or a tube of rolled up currency.

Heroin has made a recent resurgence in popularity, due mainly to availability and low prices. Among eight heroin overdose deaths reported in the Denver area, during a three-month period in the fall of 2001, two were students.

Narcotic Analgesics

Other narcotic analgesics, or painkillers, include Demerol, Percodan, and Darvon-N, all usually available in pill form as prescription drugs. Because these drugs are prescribed, they can be found in the medicine cabinet in many homes. Teens will frequently take these pills from a parent's medicine cabinet and use them or sell them. There are also adults with access to these medications who will sell them on the street. Overdose from narcotics is sometimes due to the buyer not knowing what he or she is really getting. The drug may be very pure, therefore stronger than what the buyer is used to. The buyer may take his or her usual amount of the substance and be getting more than he or she asked for. This was the case with China white, a street name for heroin that was used to market fentanyl, a synthetic narcotic with ten times the potency of heroin. The potential for physical addiction from all of these drugs is very high.

The most recent opiate to be abused is OxyContin, a slow-release painkiller whose active ingredient is oxycodone (Percolone, similar to Percodan). Many recreational drug users who avoid heroin because of its negative connotations are drawn to Oxy-Contin. Abusers of this opiate can achieve a euphoric heroin-like high by crushing the tablets and then either snorting or cooking down and injecting the contents. Information from medical examiners across the country has linked the drug to more than 300 overdose deaths in thirty-one states, including Maine, where abuse of this substance has become an epidemic.

What it feels like to be high on an opiate. Euphoria and a sense of general well-being are most commonly reported with opiate use. Incidentally, the term "heroin" was originally coined in 1898 to describe an improved version of morphine. It was used as a brand name by the Bayer (aspirin) company and was derived from the German word "heroisch," meaning to feel large or heroic.

Behavioral indicators. Physical signs of use include needle marks and tracks. "Pinned" eyes (small pupils) indicate a drugged state, and the user has a tendency to nod (appear very drowsy and non-responsive to external stimuli). Withdrawal looks very much like having the flu; symptoms include nausea, vomiting, diarrhea, restlessness, and muscle aches. Narcotic withdrawal may be very uncomfortable, but it is not life threatening.

Depressants

Depressants are a class of drugs that depress the functions of the central nervous system.

Alcohol

Let's start with ethyl alcohol (beer, wine, vodka, gin, scotch). Amazingly, many parents are just beginning to realize that alcohol is indeed a drug. Meanwhile, underage drinking has grown to epidemic proportions. In fact, alcohol is the number one drug of abuse for American teens. Since the end of Prohibition, this drug is now legal for adults, but far from being safe, it is in reality the most deadly drug currently being used by our society. Alcohol is a major factor in the three leading causes of teen death: driving accidents, suicide, and homicide.

Alcohol depresses the central nervous system. Doses of less than two ounces of ethyl alcohol—two hard-alcohol drinks, or two twelve-ounce bottles of beer, or two four-ounce glasses of wine—per day result in blood alcohol levels of below 0.05 percent and produce a feeling of relaxation and well-being. Anything above that has negative consequences, including general anesthesia, coma, and, at extremely high levels, respiratory depression leading to death. The amount of alcohol needed to produce these effects depends on the body weight of the person and on their particular metabolism. Overdose potential is high because alcohol tolerance increases with continued use. There is evidence of both psychological and physical dependence.

By the way, a forty-ounce bottle of Old English beer (actually an ale), with high alcohol content, contains the equivalent of more than five shots of hard alcohol.

Especially problematic among young people is the practice of engaging in drinking games that encourage the rapid consumption of alcohol. Another dangerous activity is the consumption of Jell-O shots, which gets a lot of highly concentrated alcohol into the body in a short period of time. (Jell-O shots are prepared by making regular Jell-O following the directions on the package. Then alcohol, usually vodka, is added instead of cold water, and the mixture is refrigerated and allowed to set in ice cube trays or small paper cups.)

Downers

Barbiturates or sleeping pills are prescription drugs that may be sold on the street. When found in the form of red capsules (Seconal), they are appropriately known as "reds." Other forms are Nembutal ("yellow jackets"), Amytal ("blue angels"), phenobarbital ("barbs"), and Tuinal ("rainbows"). These drugs have a very high overdose potential, especially when taken in combination with alcohol. That's because these drugs are *potentiated* (the effects are multiplied) by alcohol. Some adults may remember Dorothy Kilgallen of the television show *What's My Line?* who died of an accidental overdose when she took a sleeping pill after having drinks and wine with dinner. The risk of physical addiction with barbiturates is very high, and detoxification must be done carefully to avoid life-threatening seizures.

Non-barbiturate sedative hypnotics, such as Quaaludes (no longer available in the United States), Placidyl, Doriden ("goofballs"), and chloral hydrate function much like the other downers listed above. The powerful overdose potential is best demonstrated by the combination of chloral hydrate (knockout drops) and alcohol, which used to be called a "Mickey Finn."

Minor tranquilizers, primarily the benzodiazapines like Valium (which used to be known as "housewife's helper") and Librium, have a relatively small overdose potential but may be physically addictive with heavy prolonged use.

What it feels like to be high on depressants. Most people know about the effects of alcohol. The first drink or two brings relaxation and a feeling of comfort in social situations. A few more drinks and speech becomes difficult. Eventually, the room begins to spin, and it's difficult to stand up.

Basically, the effects of barbiturates and the other sedative hypnotics mentioned are very similar to those of alcohol. However, these drugs are usually more sedating (that's why they're called sleeping pills) and less likely to facilitate social interaction.

Behavioral indicators. You can detect if your child has been drinking from the smell of alcohol on his or her breath. Slurred speech, lack of coordination, and a clumsy gait are other signs. Barbiturate or hypnotic sedative use resembles alcohol abuse, but without the aroma of alcohol.

Withdrawal symptoms from alcohol abuse range from simple hangovers, including headaches, nausea, and vomiting, to full-blown d.t.'s, or delirium tremens. Symptoms of the latter may include frightening hallucinations, delirium, major convulsions, circulatory failure, and possibly death. High levels of intoxication may also produce significant memory loss, or blackouts. Withdrawal from barbiturates or sedative hypnotics looks pretty much like withdrawal from heroin addiction. However, unlike opiate withdrawal, the possibility of lethal convulsions make it very dangerous. Particularly tricky is Librium withdrawal, since the onset of withdrawal-related convulsions is delayed for five to seven days after the last dose.

Stimulants

Stimulants are thus named because they stimulate the central nervous system, causing increases in such measurables as heart rate and respiratory functioning.

Amphetamines

Amphetamines are generically known on the street as "speed," and include the related drugs, methamphetamine ("crystal meth"), and Benzedrine ("bennies"). Primarily available in pill form, these drugs may also be found as crystals that can be snorted through a straw or dissolved in solution and injected.

The most recent, and most dangerous, variant on methamphetamine is one called "ice," a clear solid that can be smoked and has been associated with long-term psychotic-like aftereffects. Whatever the form, amphetamines stimulate the central nervous system and result in increased alertness and arousal. Stimulant use also results in reduced appetite, an effect which is capitalized on by diet pill manufacturers. In large doses, amphetamines may often produce aggressiveness, paranoia, and auditory hallucinations—symptoms that are characteristic of short-term amphetamine psychosis.

Ritalin, a commonly prescribed drug used to treat attention deficit disorder in children, is known on the street as "pellets." It can be extremely dangerous if ground up and injected intravenously; components of the pill can create an embolism which may lodge in tiny blood vessels in the lung or eye, causing serious damage.

Overdose from amphetamines is possible but rare, unless they are injected and is primarily associated with impurities. You cannot become physically addicted to stimulants; there is, however, a high risk of psychological dependence.

What it feels like to be high on speed. Speed makes you feel alert and hyperaware of your surroundings; it was given to soldiers in World War II for these effects. Stimulant users report that taking these drugs makes them feel like they're in charge or on top of things.

Behavioral indicators. Physical symptoms of amphetamine use include dilated pupils, loss of appetite, overactivity, and fatigue from lack of sleep. Coming down from a speed run will cause the whole body to shut down (crash) and often produces acute depression as well.

Cocaine

Cocaine, coke, or blow (just like the movie title) is a drug extracted from the leaves of the coca plant most commonly found in South America. On the street, it is sold as a fine white crystalline powder which can be snorted or injected like heroin. When combined with heroin ("speedball") and injected, this can become very dangerous—as John Belushi realized too late.

Cocaine can also be smoked, or "freebased." Freebase cocaine was originally prepared by using ether, a very volatile substance, with sometimes disastrous results. (Richard Pryor found out about this the hard way. He was cooking up his own freebase, using ether, when the substance exploded, burning him severely.) These days cocaine is combined with ordinary baking soda and water. When heated and dried, this mixture of cocaine is changed from a chemical salt to a freebase crystalline alkaloid. That's where the term—freebase—originated. In this form cocaine is known as crack, hubba, or rock, and when smoked in a pipe, reaches the brain within seconds to create a short-lasting (three to five minutes) intense euphoric high. What goes up must come down. This high is quickly followed by an equally intense crash, characterized by depression and anxiety.

Experts argue about whether or not cocaine is a physiologically addictive drug. However, there is no question about the fact that crack cocaine acts in a highly addictive fashion. Overdose potential is high too, with lethal results.

What it feels like to be high on cocaine. Very exciting. A pounding heartbeat, blood rushing into your ears, a feeling often of euphoria are all symptoms. You can get the same feeling by going from a sauna or hot tub and jumping into a cold plunge. This is definitely a young person's drug.

Behavioral indicators. Physical symptoms of cocaine use include dilated pupils and rapid mood shifts. When the drug is snorted, it can result in a chronic runny nose. Extended use of snorted cocaine may result in nasal bleeding or even a perforated septum.

Freebase cocaine users will keep on using until they run out of money or run out of the drug. In fact, ATMs are often called "coke machines" by crack addicts who frequent them at 3:00 A.M. As with amphetamines, there are no withdrawal symptoms, aside from intense cravings for more of the drug, and a crash at the end of a run.

Nicotine

Nicotine is an addictive drug, a fact which even cigarette manufacturers have recently been forced to admit. The national Centers for Disease Control and Prevention reported in May 1997 that 3,000 kids become regular cigarette smokers every day. In addition, the report noted an alarming trend toward teen cigar use. The CDC estimated six million teenagers smoked at least one cigar within the last year. And 3.9 percent of boys and 1.2 percent of girls were reported to be frequent cigar smokers, having consumed more than fifty in the last year (CDC 1998). The average cigar is a potentially lethal source of nicotine. If broken down and the drug extracted and purified, a cigar would produce about 120 milligrams of nicotine, twice the dose necessary to kill a normal human adult. Luckily most cigar smokers don't inhale, because with this dosage inhaling could kill you. When tobacco is sniffed as "snuff" or chewed the resultant nicotine blood levels are even higher than when smoked, and the addiction is just as potent.

The American Cancer Society estimates that one in five cancer deaths is attributable to cigarette smoking. Nicotine is physically and psychologically addictive. Anecdotal reports from heroin addicts suggest that smoking cigarettes is a habit harder to kick than their drug of choice.

What it feels like to be high on nicotine. Most people report that the first time they smoked a cigarette they felt a little dizzy and slightly nauseated. Over time, people tend to feel more alert after smoking and have a decreased appetite.

Behavioral indicators. Physical indications of smoking include bad breath and nicotine stained fingers and teeth. Withdrawal symptoms include irritability, anxiety, headaches, loss of concentration, sleep disruption, tremors, and an inner feeling of hunger or emptiness. These symptoms may be reversed by resuming smoking, chewing nicotine gum, or using a nicotine patch.

Psychedelics

Psychedelics, or hallucinogens, are substances that alter perception. Any or all of the senses can be affected when these drugs are ingested.

LSD

LSD (lysergic acid diethylamide), commonly known as acid, is a chemical derivative of the ergot fungus, first produced in 1938. It was a legal drug until 1970 and is still used by authorized National Institute of Mental Health (NIMH) researchers exploring innovative treatment strategies. Classified as a hallucinogen, it has no overdose potential and does not produce physiological addiction or psychological dependency.

The late 1960s generated scare campaigns including the erroneous assertions that LSD causes "chromosome damage" and is stored in the spinal fluid for months. Resulting legislation made safe supplies of the drug virtually unattainable, which brings us to the main danger of the drug. Illicitly produced LSD, with no quality control, is subject to impurities and a variety of cutting agents (any substance added to the drug to increase the quantity and the profit). In fact, a lot of the LSD sold on the streets these days is often PCP, a much more dangerous drug (see below).

While LSD does not cause mental illness in an otherwise stable individual, it can play a role in bringing about acute and sometimes long-lasting psychological problems in susceptible people, such as teens. With a reliable source of uncontaminated LSD, however, the major contributors of bad trips ("bummers") are what is known in the drug field as "set and setting." That is, the experience is heavily determined by what you believe will happen and the conditions under which the drug is taken.

Mescaline

Mescaline is the name for the synthetic substance found naturally as an organic hallucinogen in the peyote cactus. The dried cactus, cut into buttons, may be chewed or brewed into a kind of tea. Its legal use by members of the Native American Church is protected by the Religious Freedom Restoration Act, passed in 1993.

Psilocybin is the name for the synthetic substance found naturally in the "magic" mushrooms sought and used in vision quests by the Huichol Indians. As with mescaline and LSD, there is no overdose potential, physical addiction, or psychological dependence associated with psilocybin.

The description of mescaline and psilocybin here has only academic value. Although the peyote cactus and psilocybin mushrooms are still grown and harvested, these drugs are rarely (if ever) available on the street these days. These products are, like pure THC (tetrahydrocannabinol), prohibitively expensive to market. In their place are PCP, or a combination of LSD and PCP cut with baking soda, lactose, or Jell-O powder (for color).

What it feels like to be high on hallucinogens. Effects vary depending on the drug and dose taken, but in general there is altered perception without loss of clarity (unlike with alcohol). Walls may appear to breathe. Music may take on a newer and deeper meaning, and colors may appear to be more brilliant or to have greater saturation. Even ordinary foods may produce extraordinary flavors. Occasionally the secrets of the universe appear to be self-evident.

Behavioral indicators. While under the influence of the drug, a user may have a tendency to exclaim "rad" (radical) or "dude." Of course, there are some old hippies who still exclaim "far out." Users' pupils can appear like pinheads; users may have difficulty tracking a conversation, can begin giggling uncontrollably, or can be looking out into space with big smiles on their faces. Conversely, they can look fearful, as if hearing voices (they may actually *be* hearing voices), or can stare at an inanimate object for prolonged periods of time. There are no withdrawal symptoms.

Phencyclidine

Phencyclidine (PCP), or Sernyl, known on the street as angel dust or rocket fuel, is a dissociative anesthetic with some hallucinogenic properties. It is currently used as a tranquilizer for large animals. Because it is cheap and easy to manufacture, dishonest street chemists and dealers will sell it as LSD or even MDMA. PCP is usually smoked, as laced cigarettes called "sherms," or rolled as a joint with mint leaves or parsley. Sometimes it is mixed with low grade marijuana. A "rocky road" is PCP mixed with crack cocaine and smoked in a glass pipe—a particularly nasty combination.

There is a definite overdose potential and, with extended use, the possibility of physical addiction. PCP's effects are dose related and highly unpredictable, including muscle rigidity, numbness, and violent outbursts. There is a higher likelihood of bad trips with PCP than with other psychedelics, and people on PCP are also harder to talk down.

What it feels like to be high on PCP. At low doses there may a combined stimulant and psychedelic effect. Higher doses can cause disorientation, agitation, and insensitivity to pain.

Behavioral indicators. A person under the influence of PCP may have a blank stare and appear to be detached from what's going on around him. There are no effects from withdrawal.

Inhalants

Inhalants are a classification of drugs that are inhaled by the user. They are synthetic solutions, usually available for other legal uses. They may be sniffed after spraying or pouring them onto a rag or into a paper bag.

Nitrites

Amyl nitrite ("poppers") and butyl nitrite ("rush") are short-acting drugs that produce a brief high, one to two minutes in duration. This is due to the drugs' ability to produce a short-term drop in blood pressure and dilation of the arteries. Also known as "smelling salts," these drugs can be used to revive someone knocked unconscious, such as an athlete.

According to anecdote, poppers prolong the sensations of sexual climax, perhaps as a result of the distorted sense of time associated with decreased oxygen flow to the brain. Research has shown that these drugs are of no benefit to people with orgasmic problems, nor are they helpful in the treatment of sexual problems in general.

Despite scare stories, there is no truth to the assertion that poppers can cause glaucoma, although they make the existing pressure felt by glaucoma sufferers even more severe. There is a potential for overdose, especially when combined with alcohol or stimulants such as cocaine and amphetamines. Users can become momentarily unconscious, and they can have a significant drop in blood pressure; in combination with alcohol or stimulants, poppers can cause significant effects on the heart. Poppers are not physically addictive, but regular users can build up tolerance to the drug.

What it feels like to be high on poppers. The brief high is characterized by a flushing sensation as well as a feeling of light-headedness, relaxation, and mild euphoria.

Behavioral indicators. Possession of glassine ampoules. There are no withdrawal effects.

Glue and Chemo

Glue sniffing has risen to epidemic proportions among the street kids of South and Central America (particularly in Honduras). In industrialized countries, such as the United States, the inhalant of choice is "chemo" or "o.b." These terms refer to products used as gasoline octane boosters and can be found in any automobile accessory store.

Huffing, or sniffing a chemo-soaked rag in a paper or plastic bag, was shown in the movie, *My Life as a House*. Toluene, which is present in substances such as paint thinner, is a volatile anesthetic solvent, and high concentrations in the circulatory system may lead to permanent brain damage. The overdose potential is high.

When inhaled, paint thinner, glue, lighter fluid, and so on cause a rush of adrenaline to the heart and can cause cardiac arrest and "sudden sniffing death." These drugs are not physically addictive, but users can build up tolerance to them and develop a mild psychological dependency.

What it feels like to be high on glue or chemo. When inhaled, these drugs produce a rapid central nervous system depression characterized by exhilaration, dizziness, floating sensations, and intense feelings of well-being.

19

Behavioral indicators. Possession of unusual or unwarranted amounts of glue or automotive products. There are no effects from withdrawal.

For information on designer, club, and rave drugs, such as ecstasy and GHB, see chapter 3.

CHAPTER 2

Putting Drugs in Perspective

Anthropologists studying other cultures, both historically and contemporarily, have found that most people use something to alter their consciousness some of the time. Using plants, their roots, or processes that turn something edible into something intoxicating, most cultures have found a way to get high. Civilizations in ancient Mesopotamia brewed a type of beer. The indigenous Yanomamo tribe, living by the Amazon River in South America, snorts a green paste through a tube. Certain Native American tribes ingest peyote or the magic mushroom. Whether used for rituals, religious ceremony, or to relieve pain, drugs have been used by most cultures as a way to get "stoned." There is something naturally compelling for all humans about the altered feeling achieved. Think of a child's dizzy delight, after twirling around as fast and as long as she or he can.

And what about *our* culture? Movies, television, and advertising have made it clear that using drugs and alcohol is an integral part of how we live. Mind-altering substances have achieved a level of normalcy for us. Whether it's taking a pill to relieve pain or tension, or having a drink to relax, we use substances on a regular basis. Many people begin using mind-altering substances in adolescence. You, yourself, may have experimented with drugs or used alcohol or other drugs regularly as an adolescent. It's not so surprising, then, that drug use has infiltrated our children's lives.

All teenagers use drugs. Ask any high school student and that's what they'll tell you. And many teens do not perceive the use of drugs as presenting any great risk. The availability of drugs is greater now than at any time since the late 1970s. The good news is that not *all* teens are using drugs (and we include alcohol in this category). The bad news is that that there is still cause for real concern. The number of teens who have access to alcohol and other drugs is alarming. We hope that you, as a parent, will focus closely on the problems of adolescent substance use, not only for your own teen but for all the teens in the community in which you live.

We believe that the best tool for understanding and combating the problem of adolescent alcohol and drug use is information. Becoming aware and informed will keep you from being left behind as your teen negotiates his/her way along the difficult path to adulthood.

Stages of Adolescent Substance Use

There are four distinct stages, or degrees, of teen use of alcohol and other drugs; each stage of use can lead to the next:

- experimentation

- regular use or misuse

- abuse

- dependence or addiction

Although these stages are distinct, it is not easy to identify an exact time or event that can move a teen from one stage of use to the next. Experts in the drug treatment community refer to this fuzzy progression from one stage to the next as the "invisible line" that a teen crosses as their drug or alcohol use continues. As the teen crosses this line, both the teen and his or her parents may believe that nothing has changed or that a teen's use has not become more alarming. No one may recognize that a progression in use (and the problems created by that use) is happening.

Adults, too, pass through similar stages of use, although the behaviors and consequences of each stage differ from those of adolescents. When adults struggle with substance-abuse problems, their behavior can look similar to what we see in the adult population as a whole and can therefore seem natural or at least acceptable. Many adults have indulged in alcohol and drug use and have perhaps had "a few too many" once or twice. Adults with substance-abuse problems can often hide their drinking or drug use, at least for a while.

When adults do begin to have negative consequences, the problem is usually difficult to ignore or deny. Consequences may be quite severe, especially as drug or alcohol abuse continues over a period of years. Many addicted adults are faced with losing their jobs, their marriage, or their health. These negative consequences are often what forces an adult to finally seek help. This is called "hitting bottom," when there is no way but up from the problems caused by drinking or drug use.

Luckily, teens who use drugs and alcohol usually bring attention to themselves, and the potential problems their use is creating, more quickly. Their altered behavior is harder to hide and will frequently cause the adults around them to become concerned. That's the good news. But more often, the consequences of drinking or using drugs are not as severe or dramatic for teens as they are for adults—at least not in the short run—so their use of substances may be ignored for a longer period of time and may increase or progress to more advanced stages without intervention.

After being initially concerned with the discovery that their teenaged child has been drinking alcohol or smokes marijuana, parents often retreat from doing anything about it. They try to justify or rationalize the problem away. It's tempting to think that it's just a stage, or to believe that there are lots of teens whose grades drop in high school, or to think that all teens are moody and irritable. Problems are often blamed on something or someone else and not on the drugs themselves. And frequently teens won't experience the negative consequences of their behavior because parents, teachers, and other caring adults protect them.

An even more significant difference between adults and teens is the amount of time it takes a teen, compared to an adult, to pass through the four stages of drug use. A person who begins experimenting in early adulthood may continue to use and find their use progressing in a negative way, but the progression from experimentation to addiction can take several years. An adolescent who begins experimenting with drugs and alcohol will pass through the stages much more rapidly (Clark, Kirisci, and Tarter 1998; DeWit et al. 2000).

Another alarming discovery is that the younger a teen begins using drugs and alcohol, the more likely it is that he or she will progress into addiction or dependence. Young people who begin

23

drinking before age twenty-one are more than twice as likely to develop an alcohol problem. Worse yet, teens who begin drinking before age fifteen are four times as likely to become alcoholics as those who don't drink before they're twenty-one. Even within the adolescent years, a teen who tries alcohol or marijuana at thirteen is much more likely to become addicted than a teen who begins "partying" in his or her senior year of high school (Grant 1998). Consider the profound number of physical, emotional, and cognitive changes happening in these formative years at the same time a teenager is experimenting with substances. It is no wonder that while his or her development is accelerating, so too is the development of a dangerous drug problem. And although the research outlined above begins with teens at age twelve, there is plenty of anecdotal evidence that kids as young as nine or ten years old may begin experimenting with alcohol and illicit drugs.

The following discussion of teen use of substances includes the signs and symptoms in each stage of development so that you will be better able to determine where your teen falls on the continuum.

Experimentation

Adolescents are curious beings. They have more freedom, mobility, and perceived independence than they did when they were young children. They have heard about drugs, and they have seen adults and older teens using alcohol and perhaps other substances. It is natural for their curiosity about new and different experiences to extend to finding out what the big deal is about alcohol and other drugs. Not all teens experiment with substances in order to satisfy their curiosity, but it's clear from current research that most teens in this country will try alcohol or marijuana at some time.

Experimentation is usually marked by unplanned, infrequent use of substances in small amounts. Teens who use at this stage usually do so for the thrill of acting grown up and defying their parents. It is part of the "high." They usually don't need very much of the substance (one beer or a couple "hits" of a joint) to feel the effects; in other words, they have low tolerance.

There are usually few, if any, negative consequences to such experimentation. Experimenting teens become aware of the mood-changing effects and learn to moderate their doses to achieve a desired level of mood alteration or high. Once a user has learned this, the "experiment" is over, and the next intoxication is a planned and desired experience.

Tobacco, alcohol, and marijuana are the most common first substances used by teens. These three substances are considered "gateway" drugs. They are the most widely used drugs among teens across the nation and are the easiest for them to find and use. They are called gateway drugs because teens who start with them are introduced to people and places where other substances are used. Once a teen experiments with one of the gateway drugs, they are more likely to try hallucinogens, amphetamines, cocaine, heroin, or other drugs. In fact, the use of tobacco, alcohol, or marijuana increases the chances, but the use of two, and particularly the use of all three of these substances, significantly increases the likelihood of a teen going on to try other illicit drugs. Experimenting with all three gateway drugs also significantly increases the likelihood of progressing to the next stage, which is regular use or misuse.

Not all teens who use the gateway drugs will go on to use other drugs. Many teens continue to use only alcohol or marijuana. Many teens stop using drugs altogether after the experimentation period ends. Unfortunately, many other teens do not or cannot stop at this point.

Regular Use or Misuse

Teens who continue to use substances more than a few times are no longer experimenting. They may try new or different substances and think they are still experimenting, but continued use of any substance means they have moved to the next stage of use.

In this stage, use becomes more regular and frequent. Regular use requires planning. The teen is still exerting control and choice. His or her consumption usually increases, often along with pride in being able to "handle" the high. With teens, there is often a perception that "everyone does it" and the feeling of wanting to be in with the crowd.

Use will occur on weeknights rather than just on weekends. Sometimes teens will begin using alone and not just in social situations. They begin buying alcohol or drugs, therefore needing money, false IDs, and older friends to help them get their supply.

There are generally few negative consequences to their using, though this is frequently the time when parents become aware of their behavior and may impose consequences at home. Teens may begin lying to parents about the extent of their use ("I've only tried it once") and make excuses for any information parents may have discovered ("It wasn't my beer. I was keeping it for a friend"). Their grades may drop, and they may cut down on extracurricular activities.

Abuse

When teens are still in the stage of regular use/misuse, they continue to be involved in most of their usual activities and interests. When alcohol and drugs are used, it is often to enhance or accompany an activity. The activity is still the focus. When a teen progresses to the stage of abuse, however, the activity is no longer primary. The drugs or alcohol are what's important and the activity loses its meaning. Previously, a teen might enjoy getting stoned to see a really great movie or drink a few beers before the football game. Once a teen moves into the stage of abuse, getting to the movie theater or the game is secondary to getting high. Using drugs becomes the activity itself, and nothing else seems as fun or important.

The teen becomes preoccupied with using, and solitary use increases. Teens may isolate themselves from other non-using friends. Being high becomes normal and non-using friends are frequently dropped. They may make promises to friends or themselves to cut down or quit but find themselves unable to do so. They may feel depressed or have suicidal thoughts as they begin to recognize the vicious cycle their use has put them in. But still, they're unable to stop.

The number of times during the week that they use increases. The amount of money spent for drugs increases as well. They may have to conceal where the money is coming from and where it is going. Selling, or dealing, as a way to get money or drugs for free begins. Teens in this stage may steal money from parents or friends. Use of harder drugs increases.

Increased tolerance is a sign of abuse. Teens will need more and more of the substance to get the desired effect. Perhaps two to three beers once got them drunk, but once they've moved to the stage of abuse, it will take a six-pack or more to get the same feeling. Similar tolerance will occur with other substances. The increase in the amount of a drug needed to get high contributes to the negative physical and psychological effects the substance may bring.

When a teen moves into this stage, the negative consequences of use become harder to ignore. These consequences may parallel the devastating effects of drug and alcohol use seen in adults. There may be arrests for possession or consumption of alcohol, driving under the influence, and subsequent trouble with the courts. Probation may result. School and academic performance may not be just affected; it may be curtailed. Suspension or expulsion from school may occur as a result of being caught under the influence or in possession of drugs or alcohol on campus. Poor grades and poor school attendance may mean a transfer to another school.

Dependence or Addiction

The final stage in a teen's use of drugs and alcohol is dependence. We use the terms addiction and dependence interchangeably. This stage is marked by many of the same features and behaviors as abuse. The teen is preoccupied with using. He or she uses compulsively, or that is to say, feels a need to use. Teens at this stage will often use even when they don't mean to. Their use is much less under control. They start breaking their own codes of ethics or personal rules surrounding the use of drugs or alcohol. Self-imposed limits are broken, such as, "I'll never use during school"; "I'd never use hallucinogens, or amphetamines, or cocaine"; or "I'll never have sex with someone I'm not going to marry."

A teen's physical and psychological condition will usually decline. There may be loss of weight, more frequent illnesses, poor hygiene, and memory loss. Paranoia and guilt increases. They may experience a poor self-image and self-hatred as a result of some of their behaviors or the trouble they have experienced. Thoughts of suicide may increase as the teen experiences the roller coaster of drug highs and lows. And yet, they may still be in denial that drugs or alcohol are causing the problems they are having.

In this stage, negative consequences become more severe. A hallmark of addiction is the continued use of substances in spite of negative results. The fact that a teen has been arrested for possession of alcohol or marijuana or has had a DUI (driving under the influence) charge has no impact. Being suspended or expelled from one or more schools, or ending up in an emergency room for an overdose, does not stop them from continuing to use. Teens will try to place the blame on others: "The store clerk couldn't see what was going on. We weren't going to leave the store with the beer"; "The cops have it in for the kids these days"; "It's the school's fault for not teaching what's important."

Assessing Your Teen's Stage of Substance Use

Our experience has shown us that parents routinely underestimate the amount of drug use or the types of drugs their children are using. In our work with families struggling with issues of teen drug use, we frequently ask parents and teens to identify the stage they believe the teen is currently in. Usually we begin by asking the parents this question, and then follow up by asking the teens to rate themselves in one of the four stages. Parents will place their teen one to two stages earlier in the progression than the stage in which the teens will place themselves. Teens are surprisingly honest, once they are aware of the specific behaviors and consequences seen in the various stages. Parents are often very surprised at their child's personal assessment. Often, even after a teen admits to his or her parents the extent of substance use, parents will disagree with the teen and continue to downplay the seriousness of the drug use.

Thirty Years of Teen Drug Use

Adolescent use of alcohol and other drugs has been studied extensively over the past three decades. In the following discussion, we will separate teen use of alcohol from their use of other illicit drugs. We believe, however, that alcohol is just as much a drug as any others we report on. It is, in fact, the most widely used drug among teens and the most dangerous and damaging of all abused substances. Alcohol is frequently disregarded as a substance to be concerned about, but it is an illegal drug for anyone under twenty-one years of age. And you may be startled to see just how prevalent alcohol use among teens is in our culture. Teens are three times more likely to use alcohol than other drugs.

Two studies that have been conducted on the national level give us a wealth of information on current, as well as past, adolescent drug use. The Substance Abuse and Mental Health Services Administration (SAMHSA), within the U.S. Department of Health and Human Services, identifies national trends and provides guidelines to prevent and treat a wide variety of mental health and substance abuse issues. It oversees the work of the Center for Mental Health Services, the Center for Substance Abuse Prevention, and the Center for Substance Abuse Treatment. Since 1971, SAMHSA has conducted an annual survey on the prevalence of illicit drug, alcohol, and tobacco use in the population.

The study, entitled "The National Household Survey on Drug Abuse," examines the habits of adolescents and adults; the youngest interviewed are twelve years old. The latest (SAMHSA 2001) surveyed approximately 70,000 people; information was self-reported anonymously and the accuracy of the results was validated.

Since 1975, the National Institute of Drug Abuse (NIDA) has conducted a series of annual surveys of adolescents in public and private secondary schools. The surveys originally interviewed only twelfth graders, but since 1991, they have also included eighth- and tenth-graders. The latest survey interviewed about 45,000 students in 435 schools nationwide (Johnston, O'Malley, and Bachman 2001).

The two studies have produced very similar results. The information gathered from the NIDA and the SAMHSA studies, as well as the conclusions they draw, point to a need for more focus and attention on adolescent substance use.

Tobacco Use

Although tobacco was not considered an illicit drug when the SAMHSA surveys began in 1971, it is now classified as a drug of abuse. It is particularly important to include the statistics on adolescent use of tobacco in our discussion because of the alarming numbers of teens who smoke. We also know that those teens who use tobacco are more likely to use alcohol and other drugs than nicotine-free teens. Of the youths age twelve to seventeen who were currently smoking cigarettes at the time of the most recent SAMHSA survey, 42.7 percent also reported using illicit drugs in the previous month, compared to only 4.6 percent of non-smokers. The conclusion is obvious. If we can keep our kids from trying tobacco, it will help to keep them from experimenting with alcohol and other illicit drugs.

According to the same survey, by the twelfth grade, nearly two-thirds of all teens had tried cigarettes. It was estimated that 18.2 percent of youths age twelve to seventeen, or 4.1 million teens, were current cigarette smokers in 2000. By twelfth grade, 31 percent were current smokers. Even as early as eighth grade, 41 percent had tried cigarettes and 15 percent were current smokers.

The rate of tobacco use has remained relatively stable since 1980. Use began to rise in 1992 and reached its peak in 1996 (for eighth- and tenth-graders) and 1997 (for twelfth-graders) but has fallen since that time. In 2000, there appeared to be a significant decline in smoking for all three grades. The NIDA study attributes this decline to increases in perceived risk of smoking and disapproval of tobacco use. In addition, it has become increasingly difficult for younger teens to get cigarettes over the past four years. Education efforts in the media and in schools may finally be working!

Alcohol Use

According to the most recent SAMHSA survey, 9.7 million current drinkers were ages twelve to twenty. That figure represents almost one-third of that age group in the U.S. There have been no statistically significant changes in the rates of underage drinking since 1994. Four out of five teens (80 percent) use alcohol by the end of high school. About half (52 percent) of all teens do so by the eighth grade. Information from the most recent SAMHSA survey indicates that the area of most concern is binge drinking. Two-thirds of the group, or 6.6 million, engaged in binge drinking (meaning they drank five or more drinks on one occasion) and an additional 2.1 million would be classified as heavy drinkers (meaning they had five or more drinks on one occasion five or more times in a thirty day period).

In addition to studying percentages of alcohol use among teens, the NIDA study also asked teens what they thought the risk was in using alcohol and other drugs. The risk of using alcohol was perceived differently by twelfth-graders than by eighth- and tenth-graders. According to the 2000 NIDA study, twelfth-graders do not view binge drinking as being much of a risk, and that view has not changed much over the twenty-year period that the study has been conducted. However, between 1986 and 1992, that view did change slightly, with a steady rise in those surveyed (from 36 percent to 49 percent) believing that binge drinking carried a great risk. Among the eighth- and tenth-graders, only studied since 1991, between 52 and 58 percent consider binge drinking risky. The NIDA study also surveyed teens' attitudes about drinking alcohol and using illicit drugs. The number of teens who disapprove of binge drinking corresponds to the number of teens who view binge drinking as posing a risk. According to the survey's authors, the results indicate some success from the drunk drinking campaign and the notion of a designated driver. It does appear that alcohol is still viewed as fairly easy to obtain. Just fewer than 90 percent of tenth-graders and just fewer than 100 percent of twelfth-graders perceive alcohol as fairly easy or very easy to get. Only among eighth-graders has the perception of the availability of alcohol decreased in the last four years.

Another study, released in early 2002, was conducted by the National Center on Addiction and Substance Abuse (CASA) at Columbia University to examine underage drinking. While results from this study are generally comparable to the previous studies, one alarming new finding is that teens are starting to drink at younger ages. Since 1975, the number of teens who began drinking in the eighth grade or earlier has risen from 27 to 36 percent (Foster and Richter 2002).

Illicit Drug Use

At the beginning of the twenty-first century the problems of teen drug abuse remain. Today over half of all teens have tried an illicit drug by the time they finish high school. Based on the NIDA findings, the rate of drug use was higher in the late 1970s. In 1979, 66 percent of all teens had tried an illicit drug; that rate declined to a low of 41 percent in 1992, and rose back to 54 percent in the year 2000.

According to the NIDA study, illicit drug use among twelve- to seventeen-year-olds declined slightly between 1997 and 1998, and then leveled off. In 2000, the only age group which showed a decline in use was the twelve- to thirteen-year-olds. This decline in use is attributed primarily to the decreased use of inhalants by this age group.

In the 2000 study, an estimated 1.1 million youth age twelve to seventeen met the diagnostic criteria for dependence on illicit drugs.

Marijuana is the most widely used illicit drug among teens, so questions about its use were asked separately. Marijuana use peaked in 1979 at 51 percent among twelfth-graders and then declined throughout the 1980s. In the 1990s marijuana use rose again, peaking in 1996 and only slightly decreasing since then. Marijuana is widely available at all grade levels with increasing availability as teens get older.

New information from SAMHSA since the last survey also indicates that adolescent admissions for addiction treatment have increased because of marijuana use. Between 1994 and 1999, the number of adolescents admitted to substance-abuse treatment programs increased by almost 20 percent. During that time, admissions for marijuana use increased from 43 percent to 60 percent of all adolescent admissions to drug treatment programs. And over half of those admissions came from referrals through the criminal justice system (SAMHSA 2001).

Trends in Use of Illicit Drugs and Alcohol

An alarming number of teens have used drugs and alcohol over the past thirty years. According to the NIDA research, the rates are much higher than at any other point in U.S. history as well as significantly higher than elsewhere in the world. In the latest survey, almost one-third (29 percent) of twelfth-graders had tried an illicit drug other than marijuana.

By 1975, the majority (55 percent) of teens had used an illicit drug by the time they left high school. The figure rose to 66 percent by 1981 and then declined to 41 percent in 1992. Currently the rate of illicit drug use is back to 54 percent. Binge drinking reached its peak in 1979, about the same time as the use of illicit drugs did. There was also a decline in alcohol use in the 1980s, reaching a low of 28 percent in 1992. However, alcohol abuse has risen as well; one-third of all teens engage in binge drinking.

There also have been some increases in the use of certain drugs. MDMA or ecstasy use showed the largest increase among students. In the last two years of the NIDA study there was a dramatic increase in the number of twelfth-graders who reported using ecstasy in the previous twelve months. The figure rose from 5 to 8 percent. A study conducted by the Partnership for a Drug-Free America in 2001 found that of the 6,937 twelve- to eighteen-year-olds surveyed, 12 percent had used ecstasy sometime in their lives (Roper ASW 2001). Amphetamine and methamphetamine use also increased, according to the latest NIDA survey. In 1999 and 2000, steroid use showed a significant increase among younger male teens. Roughly 2.5 percent of eighth-grade boys and 2.8 percent of tenth-grade boys indicated some steroid use in the prior year, up from 1.6 percent and 1.9 percent, respectively.

Recently, teens reported a decrease in the use of certain illicit drugs. According to the last NIDA study, the use of inhalants, crack cocaine, and Rohypnol all decreased in 2000. Some of this decrease was a continuation of a longer-term decline. Inhalant use has declined in recent years. Rohypnol, the so-called "date rape drug," showed a slight decline in use in all three grades studied. Crack cocaine use showed a decline in 1999 and 2000.

Subgroup Differences

Trends can also be tracked by subgroups. Differences in gender, race/ethnicity, regions of the country, and populations from rural and urban areas were looked at separately in the latest NIDA and SAMHSA studies.

Gender

The study found that males are more likely to use alcohol and illicit drugs than females. They also use more steroids. Cigarette smoking appeared to be about the same for boys and girls, although boys use smokeless tobacco more. In the SAMHSA study, boys and girls showed similar rates of use for other drugs. Boys indicated a slightly higher rate of marijuana use and girls indicated a higher rate of non-medical use of psychotherapeutics. Females found it easier to get illicit drugs than males did. In the CASA study, males and females in the ninth grade were just as likely to use alcohol (Foster and Richter 2002).

Ethnicity

The NIDA study reports that among the three largest racial/ethnic groups—whites, African-Americans, and Hispanics—African-Americans indicate substantially lower use of illicit drugs, alcohol, and cigarettes than do whites or Hispanics. Use among Hispanics tends to fall between the other two groups, except in the lower grades, where their use of illicit drugs and alcohol is highest. The study suggests that Hispanics may be more precocious about trying drugs. The study also speculates why Hispanics rate of use decreases in the higher grades. The number of Hispanic youth being included in the study of older teens is smaller than that in the lower grades. Since they begin using earlier than the other two groups, they may develop a serious drug problem and drop out of school before the twelfth grade. Those Hispanics who were studied in the twelfth grade did indicate higher rates of use of ecstasy and crack cocaine.

The racial/ethnic group with the lowest rates of use was Asians. The group with the highest rate of use was American Indian/Alaska natives.

College Plans

Teens who plan to attend college have lower rates of use than teens who are not college-bound. Teens who focus on getting an education and apply themselves to their studies are less likely to use drugs than their less studious counterparts.

Geographic Area

The South has the lowest rates of illicit drug use among teens, and the West and the Northeast have the highest. These two areas had by far the highest rates in the 1980s, with the rise of cocaine use. And the Northeast had the highest rates when the use of ecstasy increased. However, as the popularity of cocaine continued to increase and then ecstasy came on the scene, the entire nation saw an upsurge of use. The West has consistently had the lowest rates of cigarette use.

Population Density

There are no consistent differences in patterns or amounts of use between urban and non-urban areas. Although rates of use may have been higher initially in urban areas, use has decreased in cities, and non-urban areas have caught up rather quickly, in many cases, exceeding use seen in urban areas.

Trends by Decade

Trends over the last thirty years can also be looked at by decade.

The 1970s

Although teens were experimenting with many substances before the 1970s, there is no accurate data on their use of alcohol or illicit drugs.

We know there was a steady increase in the use of illicit drugs throughout the 1970s. According to the NIDA study, the only two illicit drugs with a slight decrease in use were LSD and heroin. There was also a decrease in the use of prescription drugs, such as tranquilizers and barbiturates, perhaps because the availability of illicit drugs became so much greater. The use of alcohol remained fairly steady, at around 40 percent, throughout the 1970s, with only a slight increase in use. But the use of all other illicit substances, such as marijuana, inhalants, cocaine, and amphetamines, was on the rise.

The largest increase was in the use of marijuana. Between 1975 and 1979, teen use of marijuana increased from 40 percent to over 50 percent of teens who reported using it within the past year. Cocaine also gained in popularity, increasing from 5.5 percent to over 12 percent of teens using within the past year.

During this time, the percentage of teens who perceived the use of illicit drugs and alcohol as posing a risk decreased. Even LSD, whose use decreased, was viewed by teens as not posing a great risk. Disapproval ratings for the use of these substances also decreased during this time.

The 1980s

The NIDA study found a decline in the use of all substances, with the exception of inhalants, in the 1980s. The decline in use was even sharper than the increase had been in the 1970s. There was a reduction by 8 percentage points in the use of alcohol, a significant 20 percent decrease in the use of marijuana, a complete reversal of cocaine use from 12 percent to 5 percent, a 15 percent reduction in the use of amphetamines, and a slight reduction of 2 percent in the use of alcohol. LSD use declined to just 4 percent, and heroin use remained fairly constant at .5 percent.

Corresponding to this declining trend were heightened perceptions of the risk of use. Perception of marijuana being a great risk increased from 50 percent to 78 percent of teens, cocaine from 32 percent to 60 percent, and alcohol from 38 percent to 46 percent. Disapproval ratings also increased to over 90 percent for marijuana, LSD, cocaine, and heroin. Disapproval ratings for use of alcohol by teens also increased by 10 percentage points, from 58 percent to 68 percent of teens.

The 1990s

Unfortunately, the 1990s reversed the trend of the 1980s and showed an increase in the use of illicit drugs. This reversal was reflected in both the SAMHSA and NIDA studies. The past decade revealed alarming new facts about use by younger teens. And new drugs came on the drug scene that had not been studied in past decades.

As we look back over the thirty-year trends in use of drugs by adolescents, it appears that we are right back where we started, when teen use was first studied in the 1970s. With all the ups and downs in statistics, levels of use appear to be right where they were in 1975 for twelfth-graders. After a steady decline of marijuana use in the 1980s, there was a resurgence of use with a steady increase to 1999. Although the level of use among teens was not quite up to the peak it reached twenty years earlier in 1979, it remained at around 40 percent over the last three years of the past decade. Similarly, the use of cocaine was right where it was in 1975.

Interestingly, some drugs saw a rise in use by the middle of the decade and since then saw a slight decline in use. Inhalants, LSD, amphetamines, heroin, and even cigarettes reached a peak of use in 1995, and then began a decline back to earlier levels of use. In each of these cases, levels are close to those found in the 1970s.

Alcohol is the one drug of abuse that has remained fairly constant over the past thirty years. With only a slight decrease in use since the 1970s, alcohol use among twelfth-graders remains at around 30 percent. (Please be aware, this statistic measures regular use by teens who drink five or more drinks in a row.)

Beginning in the 1990s, the NIDA study gathered information on the use of substances by younger teens. Although the use of most substances by both eighth- and tenth-graders remains lower than twelfth-graders, we see very similar patterns of use during the 1990s to the patterns seen in twelfth-graders. Marijuana use increased and then leveled off for the last three years of the decade for both eighth- and tenth-graders. Similarly, there was a steady increase in the use of cocaine. And as with older teens, we saw a pattern of increased use until 1995 and 1996 of LSD, tranquilizers, and cigarettes, with some decline after that.

Younger teens are using certain drugs more than twelfth-graders. Inhalants are used most by eighth-graders, peaking at 12 percent in 1995. Tenth-graders' use of inhalants peaked at 10 percent. Amphetamines and heroin also show this trend, with eighth- and tenth-graders using more than twelfth-graders.

The 1990s brought us statistics on new drugs such as ice and MDMA (or ecstasy). According to the NIDA study, ice showed an increase in use from about 1.5 percent of twelfth-graders using it in 1990 to 3 percent using it in 1996 and then showed a decline in 1999 to 2 percent. Although MDMA (ecstasy) was actually introduced to the drug scene in the late 1970s, its use was not studied until the 1990s, when it became more popular. Tenth- and twelfth-graders, especially, were using ecstasy in alarming numbers at the end of the 1990s. Although it has not reached the numbers seen with many other substances such as marijuana, alcohol, or cocaine, its use appears to be on the rise.

The information contained in this chapter is an overview of the state of adolescent drug use in the United States in the beginning of the twenty-first century. Specific information on teen drug use in your community, including prevalence of use, types of substances used, and resources for assistance may be available through professionals in the medical field, through your local government, through the school district, through religious organizations, and from other parents. It is crucial—it is your job as a parent of a teenager—to find out what is going on out there.

CHAPTER 3

Designer, Rave, and Club Drugs

"5 Knocked Out After Taking Designer Drugs"
—*Los Angeles Times*

"Ecstasy 'Epidemic' Alarms Authorities"
—*Greenville News*

"Teenagers at Raves at Risk for Dangerous Drugs"
—*Reuters*

"Light Ecstasy Use Might Harm Brain, Study Suggests"
—*Associated Press*

"Many Ravers Don't Know What Drug Caused Overdose"
—*Los Angeles Bureau*

If you've seen the recent news stories about teens using designer drugs at rave events, you may have been both alarmed and confused. "What are these drugs?" you may ask. "And what's a 'rave' anyway?"

The Scene

Raves are large-scale gatherings usually staged in settings like an abandoned warehouse, a loft, or even an open field. Raves are all-night dancing parties that get going in the early evening and keep going until well after midnight. The main attraction is loud, hard dance club or "techno" music with its pulsating beat—and drugs. Lots of drugs.

Raves originated in England, in the countryside around London and Manchester, over a decade ago. The idea quickly spread to the United States, where raves started as impromptu last-minute events advertised by word of mouth. These days they've become big business. Promoters advertise raves in specialty record and alternative clothing stores, at local universities, and even on high school campuses.

What does a rave look like? Picture a hot, stuffy, and dimly lit dance floor. Colorful lights overhead are lashed by computerized lasers and intermittent strobe lights. Ultraviolet lights pick out Day-Glo highlighted faces on the revelers, a sweaty group of frenetically dancing kids and young adults. Many of them are waving plastic glowsticks in the air while others dance, make out, or bump and grind, simulating sex.

And the sound. Deejays keep the crowd moving to a loud, throbbing beat. Think reggae, mixed with hip-hop and electronic elements. The music is so loud that many dancers use earplugs to prevent permanent damage to their hearing.

The Drugs

Many of the substances used at raves fall under the category of designer drugs, which were first produced in the early 1900s following an extensive chemical analysis of the hallucinogenic drug mescaline. Once the underlying molecular structure of mescaline was understood, chemists known as psychopharmacologists experimented with creating minor variations on the theme. By tweaking the original molecular chain, adding a radical here or there, they were able to design new drugs with similar hallucinogenic effect. In the 1980s, when the U.S. Drug Enforcement Agency (DEA) began putting these drugs on a restricted list, designer chemists could simply come up with new formulas, and since the DEA classifies restricted drugs based on their molecular structure, the new drugs that resulted were perfectly legal to use.

MDMA

MDMA (methylenedioxymethamphetamine) was first created by the Merck pharmaceutical company in 1912 in Germany, to be used as a diet pill. The idea was quickly abandoned and the drug was never marketed. Its modern use began in the 1970s, when Alexander Shulgin, a biochemist with a Ph.D. from UC Berkeley, began experimenting with the drug for its basically an amphetamine with psychedelic properties. It is also considered to be an empathogen, a drug that enhances empathy. In fact, it was often used in the late 1970s (when still legal) by psychotherapists in group and couples therapy to improve communication. At low doses, and under controlled conditions, this drug can produce a state of well-being and lower your psychological defenses: ideal for psychotherapy; dangerous in uncontrolled situations.

In the 1980s MDMA became known as Adam. These days MDMA is known as ecstasy, XTC, or simply "E." When ecstasy is taken at all-night raves, in high doses, bad results are guaranteed to occur. It is common to hear of bad trips, ecstasy-induced acute toxicity, and anxiety attacks. Though rare, you even hear of overdoses resulting in death. A major problem, of course, is quality control. It is difficult to know what you're buying on the street when a drug is illegal. Drug dealers are out to make money and prey on the uninformed.

However, ecstasy even in pure or unadulterated form can have some dangerous side effects. In higher doses it tends to raise the body's internal temperature. When taken and combined with dancing all night in a crowded environment, dehydration or heat exhaustion can result.

High doses of MDMA have much the same effect as methamphetamine, which can cause teeth-grinding and tongue-biting. That's why a lot of ravers suck on pacifiers while dancing. There is also some evidence that MDMA can cause a reduction of serotonin transporters in the brain. Some ecstasy users reportedly use Prozac or other selective serotonin reuptake inhibitors (SSRIs) after MDMA use in the belief that it protects them against neurotoxicity.

Recent research done by scientists at the University of Aachen in Germany demonstrates that even recreational MDMA use can cause cognitive impairment and has long-term effects on memory. The researchers (Gouzoulis-Mayfrank et al. 2000) did a study comparing a group of ecstasy users to two other groups, one drug-free, and the other marijuana smokers. The groups were carefully matched in age range and educational level. The ecstasy and marijuana users were asked to abstain for three weeks, and everybody in the study passed urine tests. The subjects were all given several hours of psychological testing to evaluate a wide range of cognitive functioning. Interestingly, the marijuana smokers performed no differently from the drug-free group.

The ecstasy group performed just as well as the two other groups on simple tests of alertness. When it came to tasks involving attention, memory, and learning, however, the ecstasy group performed worse. The more ecstasy the subjects had used, the worse their performance on the tests.

Sometimes MDMA is taken in combination with LSD. This is called "candy flipping"; add another ingredient, psilocybin, and it's called "rainbow flipping." When MDMA is taken with ketamine (see below) and methamphetamine, the combination is known as "trail mix." There's always a potential risk in combining drugs, especially when quality and quantity are unknown factors. Add some alcohol and bad results are very likely to occur.

Caution: With high doses of MDMA, there is a real potential for overdose, sometimes resulting in heart attacks and death.

GHB

Gamma hydroxybutyrate, also known as "great bodily harm" or "Georgia homeboy," has nothing in common with MDMA, despite the fact that it's often called "liquid X." Classified as a sedative-hypnotic and central nervous system depressant, it was originally developed as a sleep aid. It is colorless, odorless, and practically tasteless as well, especially when mixed with a beverage.

In low doses GHB has a mild euphoric effect, much like alcohol, making the user feel relaxed. In high doses it makes the user feel dizzy and sleepy. Overdoses can cause unconsciousness, coma, dangerously low breathing, and slowed heartbeat.

Passing out on GHB is potentially life threatening. Mixing GHB with alcohol or other depressants is extremely dangerous and has been known to cause death due to respiratory failure. GHB is extremely addictive. Regular use can cause physical dependency with harsh withdrawal symptoms, including lethal seizures.

GHB, also known as "easy lay," has also become the drug of choice for sexual predators who use it as a date rape drug. A few drops slipped surreptitiously into a drink is all that it takes to knock her/him out for a few hours. The victim awakes the following morning with memory loss similar to an alcohol blackout.

Since GHB is sometimes used as a body-building drug, this is an opportunity to mention anabolic steroids, used for the same purpose. These drugs, which include testosterone and oxymetholone, are known as "'roids" on the street. (Note: Steroids are not club or rave drugs. They are used legally by some athletes. Although there is no short-term buzz, some users report a feeling of increased energy and competitiveness after a few weeks of taking the drug. Although there is no true withdrawal effect, long-term users of steroids have reported a feeling of depression after stopping the drug.)

Caution: It is dangerous to drive while high on GHB. A single dose has the effect of five or six drinks of alcohol and can seriously impair motor coordination.

GHB Analogs

GBL (gamma butyrolactone) and BD (1,4 butanediol) are both chemicals that turn into GHB once ingested. They are sometimes sold under the guise of "natural cleaners" and promoted as safe alternatives to GHB. The product claims include stimulating growth hormone, relieving anxiety, reducing stress and depression, aiding in muscle building, enhancing athletic performance, and even combatting aging.

Common street names for GBL include blue moon, blue nitro, and rejoove. Street names for BD include FX, GHRE, serenity, thunder nectar, white magic, and zen.

Caution: Anyone driving a vehicle under the influence of one of these substances is putting themselves at great risk for an accident. These substances are also known to be physically addicting, and withdrawal effects can be life threatening.

Ephedrine

Ephedrine is an herbal stimulant. It is the active ingredient in Mahuang, a Chinese drug long used to alleviate the breathing problems associated with asthma. It is now sold on the street as herbal (or natural) ecstasy, a supposedly "safer" form of MDMA. Ephedrine is often marketed in weight-loss products like Easy Trim, Metabolife 356, or Ripped Fuel.

While ephedrine is not dangerous in low doses, when taken in high doses (common at raves) it can produce a variety of adverse health effects. Headaches, high blood pressure, insomnia, heart attacks, strokes, and seizures have all been reported in the literature. When ephedrine is taken by people who are also using MAO inhibitors prescribed by doctors for depression (Nardil, Marplan, or Parnate) the combination can be lethal.

Ketamine

Ketamine was originally marketed as Ketalar, a general anesthetic. However, it was found to produce uncomfortable hallucinations and delirium as side effects, so its medical use was discontinued. It is still currently employed as a veterinary anesthetic. Ketamine normally comes in liquid form, in small pharmaceutical bottles. Dealers dry up the liquid by cooking it, and grind the residue into a white powder.

Ketamine, known as "Special K" on the street, is now used as a recreational drug. It is often sold, mislabeled, as LSD or ecstasy. In low doses, it produces a dreamy feeling and a floating sensation. High doses of ketamine cause sensory deprivation and can produce a neurological condition that mimics a near death experience. This scary experience is known as being in the "K-hole," and is what many drug users are looking for. (Incidentally, the term was popularized by the song, "Lost in the K-Hole," recorded in 1997 by a techno-rock group called the Chemical Brothers.)

Caution: Although not physically addicting, ketamine has a high liability for psychological dependence. Frequent use can lead to serious mental disorders.

2C-B

This psychedelic designer drug, first synthesized in 1974 by psychopharmacologist Alex Shulgin, is usually classified as an enactogen (a drug which promotes getting in touch within). Current street names include "nexus," "bromo," and "cloud 9." In low doses (five to fifteen milligrams), it is mildly hallucinogenic. The visual effects of 2C-B are reportedly more intense than those produced by LSD or psilocybin. However, at even slightly higher doses it can produce nausea, trembling, and severe anxiety.

2C-B is sometimes taken in combination with MDMA and known as a "party pack." When this drug is taken in combination with LSD, it's known as a "banana split." Drug combinations like these can be particularly problematic. With no sure way of knowing what you're actually buying, or the actual dosage of the drugs, bad results are bound to occur.

Caution: The effects of 2C-B are dose related, with a few milligrams either way producing wildly different reactions. The potential for a bad trip is real and serious.

DXM

Dextromethorphan. Yes, the cough syrup. Chugalugging cough syrup, also known as "roboing" (after Robitussin), has been around for a long time. DXM in its new form, refined as a powder or transformed into pills, has greatly increased abuse potential. Unfortunately, it's now considered to be an inexpensive version of ecstasy. It does in fact mimic some of the effects of MDMA, including a sense of euphoria and hallucinations, yet can be produced at a fraction of the cost.

DXM is perfectly safe when used as a cough suppressant, in prescribed doses. In higher than prescribed doses, however, it has potent psychoactive properties. In really high doses, it can lead to terrifying trips.

This drug becomes really dangerous when combined with other drugs. When combined with an MAO inhibitor such as Nardil, or Parnate, or even the antihistamine Seldane, the results can be fatal. When combined with any of the SSRIs (Prozac, Zoloft) the result is often serotonin syndrome. This is a condition characterized by agitation, confusion, diarrhea, shivering, muscle spasms, and ataxia. The combination of DXM and nicotine has been known to produce severe nausea.

Caution: DXM is especially dangerous when combined with MDMA, as sometimes happens accidentally at raves. Both drugs are metabolized by the same liver enzyme (CYP-2D6). And since DXM inhibits sweating, the result is an increased risk of hyperthermia and heat stroke when dancing all night.

Rohypnol

Flunitrazepam is a benzodiazepine similar to Valium (but ten times more potent) and classified as a sedative hypnotic. It is manufactured by Hoffman-La Roche and sold legally in Europe and Latin America. It is not available legally in the United States but is widely used in Texas, coming across the border from Mexico.

Rohypnol is often used intentionally for the high it produces. It is, however, more notorious as a date rape drug. When even a small amount (two milligrams) is combined with alcohol, the effect is similar to a Mickey Finn. The victim is knocked out and wakes up the next day with a loss of memory.

Common street names include roofies, Mexican valium, LaRocha, roach-2, R-2, and ropies. Being under the influence of the drug is called being roached out.

Caution: While the potential for a lethal overdose is unlikely, Rohpynol is physiologically addicting. This means that true withdrawal symptoms occur after cessation of taking the drug. Headaches, muscle pains, hallucinations, shock, and cardiovascular collapse may occur. Most dangerous is that, similar to barbiturate withdrawal, convulsions or seizures may occur a week or more after the last dose. Drug detoxification with a tapering dose of another benzodiazepine is required to avoid lethal consequences.

PMA

Paramethoxyamphetamine is known as "double stacked" or "white Mitsubishi" on the street. Now here's a really dangerous drug. It is approximately twenty times more potent than regular amphetamines and extremely lethal. The real danger is that drug dealers are now selling PMA as MDMA, since it's cheaper and easier to manufacture. PMA has been known to increase internal body temperature to as high as 108 degrees.

Caution: Since 1997 there have been ten PMA-related deaths in Australia. Three PMA deaths were reported in Chicago in the spring of 1999, and six PMA-related deaths occurred in Florida in the fall of 2000. Yes, it's lethal.

Reality Check

Parents often find themselves in situations where they discover evidence of drug use by their teen. The following scenario may sound all too familiar:

Mother: Amber?

Amber: Yeah, Mom.

Mother:	Come into the living room, will you. I want to talk to you.
Amber:	Now what?
Mother:	Where were you last Friday night?
Amber:	I already told you, mom. I was studying at the library after school. Then I spent the night over at Brandi's house.
Mother:	You remember Jessica, don't you? She just started college this fall. Well, her mom called. She told me that Jessica saw you and Brandi at a weird all-night dance party in a warehouse. A "rage" event, or something like that.
Amber:	All right, Mom. We did go to the dance party. But we only stayed for a little while. And by the way, it's called a *rave*.
Mother:	Jessica was worried about you. She said that you were still there at 3:30 in the morning when she left. And that she thought you had taken some drugs, because you really looked "out of it."
Amber:	Mom! I was just dancing. I didn't do any drugs.
Mother:	Open your backpack. I want to see what you've got inside. Dump everything on the coffee table.
Amber:	Don't you trust me?
Mother:	Not anymore. Now dump it, young lady.
	[Amber upends her pack and a large variety of things spill out all over the coffee table, including a pacifier]
Mother:	What are you carrying this around for? I thought that you had outgrown this long ago.
Amber:	Oh, it's just a fad at school.
Mother:	Wait a minute. I read somewhere that a drug called ecstasy makes you grind your teeth and bite your tongue. Have you been taking ecstasy?
	[Amber responds with sullen silence]
Mother:	Amber, I want you to promise me that you'll stop hanging around with Brandi. She's a bad influence.

And swear to me that you won't go to any more of those rave things. And *never, ever* take any drugs. Is that understood?

Amber: All right, Mom, can I go now?

[Later, Amber phones her friend Brandi]

Amber: Hey Brand, I got busted by my mom. Jessica saw us at the rave and ratted us out. And my mom made me promise not to hang out with you, or go to any more raves.

Brandi: Bummer. What are you gonna do?

Amber: Well, I'll just tell her that I'm going to a late movie with Michelle. And if that doesn't work, I'll sneak out after midnight.

Harm Reduction

In the best of all possible worlds, adolescents wouldn't use or abuse dangerous illegal drugs. For that matter, they wouldn't use or abuse dangerous legal drugs, such as alcohol and nicotine, either. But we parents know that despite our best efforts sometimes our kids are just not going to listen to reason. They don't want to "just say no." The urge to experiment and peer pressure take their inevitable toll. So what's a parent to do when you know that your teen is going to raves and being exposed to potentially harmful substances?

Now is a good time to consider the option of *harm reduction*. Harm reduction is a treatment intervention being used in some drug treatment centers to minimize the harmful effects of drug use. Although within the drug treatment community, the concept is still controversial, it is gaining popularity. Originally the concept was applied to interventions with adult users who continued to use alcohol or other drugs despite negative consequences. Clean needle programs are a harm reduction concept. The idea is to reduce the potentially lethal use of these substances.

In the context of raves, we have DanceSafe. This is a non-profit, harm reduction organization based in Oakland, California, that promotes health and safety within the rave community. It has local chapters in 28 cities (more on the way) throughout the United States and Canada. (See appendix B for how to get in touch.)

According to the DanceSafe Web site, the local chapters of DanceSafe consist of trained volunteers, young people from within the rave culture, who are committed to serving their community. These volunteers are trained to be health educators and drug abuse prevention counselors.

Recently, DanceSafe provided a very valuable service to the community when they put a DXM warning on their Web site. Twelve tablets were depicted in full color, along with their street names and area of distribution. Among them was "smiley," a hexagonal pill found in Los Angeles; "star," an appropriately named star-shaped pill found in Indianapolis; "pink molly," found in Buffalo, New York; and 4-Way, found in Oakland.

Volunteers staff harm-reduction booths at raves, where they provide information on safer sex and current drugs. They also address other health and safety issues, such as using earplugs to protect hearing and having a designated driver to get home safely.

DanceSafe has also launched a campaign to encourage rave promoters to provide a "safe setting." It is well known that the vast majority of medical emergencies at raves are the result of heat stroke, a condition that is easily preventable. DanceSafe argues that reducing the heat protects the health and safety of patrons. A responsible promoter is someone who cares about more than just making money. A promoter who agrees to adopt the guidelines is given a free listing on DanceSafe Cool Promoters page.

DanceSafe points out that a safe setting should have the following characteristics:

1. Free and accessible cool drinking water.

2. Adequate ventilation (and/or air conditioning).

3. A separate chill-out room with comfortable seats.

4. A venue that's not overcrowded.

5. Secure coat-check facilities.

6. A staff member on site who is trained in first aid.

7. For large (over 500 people) gatherings, a licensed and equipped EMT (or paramedic) on site and a private room or tent where emergency cases can be treated.

8. Availability of free harm-reduction literature about drug use, safer sex, preventing heat stroke, and driving home safely.

9. Free entry to harm-reduction organizations so they can distribute literature and provide drug-abuse prevention services.

10. Enforcement of age limits when applicable.

11. The right to search patrons' outer clothes, pockets, and bags (will not admit any patron who refuses to be searched).

Perhaps the most valuable service provided by DanceSafe is on-site pill testing. This is an important harm-reduction service that reduces medical emergencies and can actually save your teen's life. It provides MDMA users a way to avoid fake and adulterated tablets that often contain dangerous substances.

Here's how it works. People attending a rave who are unsure of the authenticity of a pill they have can bring it to the DanceSafe booth. There, a trained harm-reduction volunteer will test it using a reliable reagent and be able to give accurate information.

DanceSafe volunteers are trained to follow a strict protocol for responsible pill testing. The steps are

1. Identifying and recording the pill. This includes asking for the "name" of the pill, and noting its shape, size, and color. Asking whether the pill was purchased at the event.

2. Scraping and returning the pill. A small amount is scraped from the edge of the pill onto a testing plate. The test is never performed until the pill has been returned.

3. Performing and recording the test. After adding the reagent and noting the color, either the plus sign or minus sign (indicating positive or negative) is circled.

4. Communicating the results. Many users are looking for reassurance that the pill they had tested is "safe" and "okay" to take. DanceSafe volunteers are trained to never make that kind of statement. Instead, if the test comes back positive, the owner of the pill is told that it contains real ecstasy (either MDMA, MDA, MDE, or a combination) but that these test results do not necessarily mean that the pill is "pure" or "safe." (No drug is completely safe even when pure.) The test cannot tell you how much ecstasy is in the pill. (It could be a lot or a little. You never know.)

    If the test comes back negative, the owner of the pill is simply told that it does not contain ecstasy. If the pill tests positive for DXM, the owner is cautioned about the risks involved in taking that drug, including a description of adverse reactions. He or she is also told that DXM is more likely than MDMA to cause serotonin syndrome, particularly when dancing in a hot environment.

Despite the obvious benefits, harm reduction is a controversial topic. Harm-reduction critics often complain that offering onsite pill testing is sending the wrong message to teens. They argue that the harm reduction approach condones and actually encourages the use of illicit drugs. It's clear from the above protocol that DanceSafe volunteers avoid taking a position on drug use and have never encouraged anyone to take a pill. It's also clear that the organization has saved hundreds, if not thousands, of teens from taking pills that are dangerous to ingest.

The most important thing to remember about DanceSafe is that their information and services are directed primarily to the under-served population of non-addicted recreational drug users. As a matter of policy, the volunteers are instructed to always refer people to appropriate drug treatment programs if they think treatment is needed.

So far, DanceSafe has received support from the local police in every city where it has organized a chapter, and thanks to amnesty agreements with the police, no volunteer or rave participant has ever been arrested for using the pill testing service. However, the federal government has begun a full-scale crackdown on raves and the venues where they occur, with potentially dangerous results. For example, New Orleans District Attorney Eddie Jordan filed charges against local rave promoters in 2000, accusing them of encouraging drug abuse. The list of "evidence" presented included the fact that the promoter had provided bottled water, chill rooms, and had allowed the presence of DanceSafe.

Twilo, a major nightclub in New York's Chelsea district that hosts raves, has had similar problems. In addition to making available free water and pumping cool air onto the dance floor, they even provided a private ambulance in case of overdoses or other emergencies. Incredibly, city authorities cited the availability of an ambulance as proof that the club was a "drug den." Ironically, what most people would regard as responsible behavior is now being used as proof of wrongdoing.

In California a group of local rave promoters has organized the San Francisco Late Night Coalition. This is an organization that has successfully lobbied to save many of the city's dance venues. They argue that shutting down dance venues does nothing to remove the problem of substance abuse.

In sum, the drugs described in this chapter are dangerous on many levels—first, because of the serious physical and cognitive impairments they can cause and, second, because of the lack of reliable information on the actual makeup of the drug the user is taking. It's like playing Russian roulette. What is most alarming is how many young people are using these substances. They are being marketed to teens and young adults, and they are being distributed at the kinds of parties and raves that teens attend. The information distributed by DanceSafe is not a remedy for the increasing use of these drugs. Accurate information may be a lifesaver when dealing with these newest drug additions to the scene.

CHAPTER 4

How Do Drugs Affect Teen and Family Development?

David Crosby, aging rock star and recovering addict, once spoke to a crowd of mental health and drug treatment providers about his experiences. He had gone through numerous drug treatment programs and relapsed after each program. With each year of more drugs, deteriorating health, and failed attempts to stop, his self-image and vision of his future took a nosedive. He gave up many of his life's dreams, his music suffered, and he was alone. Without questioning the negative direction his life had taken, he let the negative consequences of his drug use dictate his vision. Eventually, he landed in jail. It wasn't until he was in a cold jail cell that he finally reexamined his vision of the future. That's when he remembered the positive direction he had wanted for his life. It was only when he recaptured that positive vision that he was able to get off the downward spiral of drug use that had plagued him for years.

A similar scenario can happen to adolescents using drugs. The developing child, once filled with so much promise and possibility, can get caught in a whirlpool of negative experiences. Missing out on positive milestones can turn a teen's development in a different direction, often with devastating results.

What is meant by "development," and what does it have to do with teens using drugs? What is important about successful development for adolescents?

All living things develop over time. Plants and animals begin small and throughout their life cycle change and grow. The developmental progression depends on both environmental and individual factors, including genetic factors. Throughout the life cycle, we change, we grow. Sometimes we may regress a little, and then change and grow some more.

Individual Development

Development occurs in stages. Each stage of development occurs over a period of time and lasts until the next stage of development is reached. We begin developing in utero (the pre-natal stage), then move on to infancy, early childhood, latency, adolescence, early adulthood, and so on.

There are specific developmental tasks that must be accomplished during each stage in order to successfully move on to the next stage of development. If these tasks are not achieved, the next stage of development will be more difficult. It's like a domino effect. Lack of success in a previous stage makes it harder to successfully achieve the tasks of the next stage. For instance, an infant begins babbling with sounds like "ba-ba-ba-ba-ba." Those babbling sounds are essential in aiding a child to grow toward using words like "bottle." Eventually the baby puts words together like, "Me bottle." And finally this allows the child to say, "Hey Mom, can I have some milk?" One of the tasks of infancy is for babies to babble in order to move on to the next stage of development. This same process occurs throughout the life cycle. Mastering the tasks at each stage of development helps us to grow, mature, and succeed in the next stage of development.

Adolescent Development

Adolescence has its unique set of developmental tasks. If achieved, they will help a teen to successfully make the transition into young adulthood. These tasks include

- establishing a positive identity

- separating from caregivers

- acquiring an education

Teens who successfully accomplish these tasks will be well equipped to leave home for college or a career. They will be independent individuals, able to have healthy relationships and eventually start a family of their own. Remember, development depends on both individual and environmental factors. A variety of behaviors, activities, relationships, and experiences will help a teen with each developmental task. Let's take a look at each task of adolescence in more detail.

Establishing a Positive Identity

What does it mean to establish a positive identity? Our identity is the sum of all the experiences and relationships we encounter. The kind of person we become depends on what we think and how we feel about ourselves. How others view us is important as well, but most critical is how we view ourselves. Our beliefs, values, behaviors, how we treat others and ourselves, all shape our personal identity. As young children, our identity is very much entwined with our family's identity and how our parents relate to us. In adolescence, we begin to formulate an identity that is separate from that established in our earlier childhood. Many of the basics of what kind of person we are have already been formulated. However, many of those basics are questioned by teens and can change as a newly emerging, independent individual arises.

Teens will frequently experiment with different identities in their quest to find their true selves. Different styles of clothing, music, and activities may all be a part of this experimentation. Similarly, you may begin to see your teen associating with different kinds or groups of friends as he or she tries to figure out what feels right. The summation of all of the experiences and associations a teen encounters will help to create her or his identity.

Sometimes teens feel very uncomfortable with who they are. Many teens have told us that they don't feel like themselves, or don't feel right in their own skin. They may reinvent themselves over and over again, by changing their friends or activities or the music that they like. These changes are all part of the growth process. In fact, healthy development will include that reinvention process. Adolescents who move easily in and out of different groups of friends and interests will be more successful at discovering their true selves.

Although the Jekyll-and-Hyde character that your teen has become can drive you up a wall, it's part of your adolescent's job in order to accomplish this life-affirming developmental task. Experimentation, or trying on different hats, is a part of this task. Experimentation does not have to include the use of drugs and alcohol. However, for more than half of all teens, experimenting with substances does become a part of the process.

Separating from Caregivers

How does an adolescent separate from caregivers? As children, we are dependent on our parents for everything. In adolescence, we begin to move away from that dependence. Teens do this in many ways, some of which can drive you absolutely crazy! Teens will disagree with your beliefs and values, in an attempt to show that there is a difference between the two of you. They will ask for more freedom, begin to make their own choices, and rely less on your opinions. They will care more about what their friends think than what is on your mind. They will want to spend less time with family and more time with friends. They will want to do more things for themselves and keep more of their thoughts or feelings inside. These attempts at separation can seem somewhat extreme and often may be painful for you to endure. But your teen must exclude you in some areas in order to successfully become more independent. It is part of the process of growing up and becoming a self-reliant and responsible individual. Just keep reminding yourself that your child is doing his or her job!

Acquiring an Education

Getting an education is the third task of adolescence. This includes a formal and an informal process, both equally valuable. Formal education means all the learning that goes on in school and other religious or cultural institutions that teach teens about their world. Informal education includes all those pieces of information not taught in most schools but equally important in life. How do you negotiate with people to get what you want? How do you know when and if to trust someone? How do you present yourself in order to get a job? These are some of things that teens need to learn to become successful adults.

Acquiring a formal education is essential in today's world. The vast majority of successful adults have completed high school. Many have gone on to learn a trade, a marketable skill, or gone to college in order to begin a career. An education also helps teens accomplish the other tasks of adolescence. A teen who is a successful student thinks more positively about him- or herself, which contributes to a positive self-image.

Acquiring an informal education is equally important. As a teen separates from family and focuses more on peers and others outside of the family circle, she or he encounters opportunities to begin to discover other kinds of relationships. These include meaningful friendships, romantic relationships, and connections with other adults through work, school, sports, and other interests. As adolescents become more independent, there are also opportunities to discover how to manage money and be responsible. Acquiring these skills in adolescence will help your teen in later stages of life.

The Effects of Drugs on Adolescent Development

The stages of adolescent drug use—experimentation, regular use, abuse, and dependence—occur on a continuum. Progression on the continuum of drug use has an effect on the teen's quest for a positive identity, desire to separate from caregivers, and need to acquire an education. The further along teens move on the continuum, the more their development will be affected. When drug abuse or dependence on substances begins, development is severely compromised.

The Effects of Drugs on the Ability to Acquire an Education

The physiological effects of drug use include memory loss, difficulty concentrating, lack of motivation, and difficulty processing information. These negative effects interfere with a teen's ability to learn, and make the task of acquiring an education more difficult. A teen who is using drugs, even recreationally on weekends or in the evenings (let alone those teens who are using before and during school), has impaired his or her ability to think clearly, reason, concentrate, and memorize information. Teens who use drugs will be less motivated to focus on school and may be distracted from their studies by their desire to use. They may fall behind in their schoolwork and find it difficult to catch up. As the cycle progresses, teens frequently feel trapped. When in the grip of using drugs, they may not see that their use is to blame for their difficulties. They may decide to take less challenging courses or get off the college-bound track. They may be asked to repeat a year of high school, or they may opt to transfer to a continuation school or remedial school. They may even decide to drop out of school entirely, thinking that they just can't do the work that is expected and necessary to succeed. Those teens that stick it out and struggle to graduate from high school may have a lower grade point average, reducing their chances of getting into college.

And it is not only the lack of a diploma that is a problem. Without the actual knowledge learned in school, many teens will be handicapped as adults when it comes to dealing with the numerous obstacles and tasks set before them. Their chances of success in early adulthood, and all the stages of development thereafter, will be forever limited.

The informal education acquired during adolescence is also crucial for a successful transition into early adulthood. A teen using drugs while trying to learn all the intricacies of how our world works is at a great disadvantage. Someone who is under the influence of substances while dating, trying to get a job, or even negotiating a curfew with parents is severely handicapped in his or her ability to master these essential skills.

An example of this handicap comes from John, a thirty-year-old in an outpatient drug treatment program. He began smoking marijuana at age thirteen, and started using alcohol and cocaine by the time he finished high school. He continued to use throughout his twenties. In a treatment group in which we were discussing relationships, John reported that he had met a very nice woman at a twelve-step meeting. He wanted to ask her out and was sharing his fears with the group. How should he approach her? What should he say? How would he know what signals she was giving out? He had never had a romantic or sexual relationship with a woman without using substances of some kind, and he had no idea how to go about it clean and sober. If you were in that group and had closed your eyes and listened to his concerns, you might have thought there was a fifteen-year-old boy talking. He had never acquired the necessary skills to begin or maintain a relationship. His development in this area was crippled by his use of drugs.

The Effects of Drugs on Separation and Individuation

The second developmental task, separation from caregivers, is tricky even for adolescents not using substances. This is a vulnerable time for teens. They are trying to be independent, yet they clearly need parental support (monetary and emotional) to succeed. Teens will often push parents away, refusing assistance or guidance. An hour later, they'll come back and ask for help on a homework assignment or for money for clothes or the prom. They won't say a word about whom they are interested in romantically but may let you comfort them when a tearful breakup occurs.

If an adolescent is using drugs, the separation process becomes even more difficult. Teens using substances are easy to anger and also exhibit more isolative behavior from family. Their cries for more freedom, more independence, and a life of their own are often filled with increased hostility. The desire to have their own life is often a result of wanting to be left alone to do whatever they want, whenever they want. A parent who tries to limit a teen's activities in an attempt to curb continued use of drugs is often met with anger. And because parents are typically so fearful and worried about the drug-using behaviors, they tend to try to make the limits even stricter, and they become angry as well.

Latisha was the third and last child in her family. Her brother and sister had left home for college and careers. She always felt that her parents had "babied" her, and she was tired of it. Her dad was a recovering alcoholic with twenty years sobriety. Latisha hadn't even known her dad when he was drinking, but the family always talked about dad's alcoholism and had clear values about the dangers of drinking.

Latisha started hanging out with a new group of friends when she entered high school. They were older than she was and had later curfews and fewer restrictions than her parents imposed. They also had very different ideas about growing up. After high school, they planned to travel the world and just work here and there. Although Latisha and her family had always valued a college education, this sounded like a lot of fun. Her new friends also drank a lot of brandy and smoked a lot of weed. Latisha started to join in, questioning her dad's "fanatic" way of thinking about alcohol. She stayed away from home as much as possible, especially when she was stoned. Her parents became worried about her, but she brushed them off or told them to get out of her face. Latisha's parents even asked her older sister to talk to her, but she just told her sister to "get the hell out!"

Some of her friends were already eighteen years old and out of high school. Latisha began cutting school to be with them. One day, at a park, after she and her friends were really high, a slightly older guy approached them and asked if they had any weed. They did and agreed to sell him a dime bag (ten dollars' worth). The guy was an undercover police officer. Since several of Latisha's friends were over eighteen, they all said it was her weed. Latisha was arrested, along with her friends, and she was taken to juvenile hall where she was booked for selling marijuana. She stayed there for two weeks before going to court and being sent to a drug treatment program. Well, Latisha sure wasn't "babied" by her parents anymore. Instead, she was mistrusted, given a stricter curfew, and forced to get a job to help pay for the court costs and treatment program.

The paradox for teens is that although using drugs is a way to be separate, or different, from their parents and to exert their independence, the result is less freedom, more scrutiny, and a reduction in privileges. In addition, if teens continue to use drugs, it inevitably means less freedom in general. Poor grades may mean more school, not less. A teen caught at school or by the police for being under the influence or for possession of drugs or alcohol may have to pay court costs and serve time in jail. This tends to reduce, not increase, freedom. And having to rely on your parents to bail you out of jail, talk to your teachers, or pay any debts you may have incurred means less independence, not more.

We frequently say to teens in drug treatment programs that there are many ways to leave home. You can be given the keys to the car and have a parent help you find an apartment or dorm room and buy you the necessary essentials to start out on your own. Or you can slam the door as you leave with no forwarding address—or more likely if you've been using drugs, have the door slammed in your face because you have been kicked out of the house at age eighteen for your drug-using behavior. These are all ways of separating and leaving home. We ask the teens to choose the way that sounds easier and more appealing to them.

The Effects of Drugs on Forming a Positive Identity

The primary developmental task for teens, which is forming a positive identity, may be the most difficult for drug users to accomplish, and failure to successfully accomplish this task has the most long-lasting and devastating results. Teens who regularly use alcohol or drugs often get stuck with more limited choices of friends and interests, which limits their ability to discover themselves. They may give up activities that used to be enjoyable and that they used to feel good about.

Regular use of substances can result in poor grades and deteriorating relationships with family and friends. Substance use may also result in arrests and possible time in juvenile hall. Imagine all of these negative experiences occurring at a time when you were figuring out who you are, or how to define yourself. There will be less and less successes and more and more failures. Poor grades may lead teens to think they just aren't smart enough to succeed in school. Run-ins with the law may make them feel that the world is out to get them or that they are just someone who constantly gets in trouble. Failed relationships may lead them to believe that family and friends don't love them and that they are unlovable. They may come to believe that they can't even feel love for someone close to them. These feelings can be long lasting, following teens into early adulthood and beyond, and resulting in difficulties in all aspects of their adult lives.

Diminished beliefs about who you are can lead to a lowering of expectations for your future. The options that are available seem more limited. In order to succeed, adolescents need to have a positive vision of who they are becoming and the direction they want for their lives. Sigmund Freud believed that a healthy person succeeds in love (their relationships) and in work (which is school for teens). These give a sense of accomplishment, meaning, and purpose to life. Teens who abuse drugs are not successful at love or work, so they are less likely to have a positive vision. Then there is a downward spiral, a whirlpool that keeps sucking them down. They soon can't see a way out, can't see any good things in their future. All they can see is what is happening right now.

Many adolescents who begin using substances already have low self-esteem and turn to drugs as an escape from feelings of inadequacy. Using can be an attempt to fit in with a crowd and feel accepted. Many teens have had painful or traumatic childhood experiences that make their world one of fewer possibilities. Unfortunately, the negative consequences that accumulate while using substances can confirm a negative self-concept and a limited future. Using drugs becomes a self-fulfilling prophecy, perpetuating negative beliefs and cutting off possibilities.

Differentiating Between Substance Abuse and Other Problems

Many parents are confused about their teen's substance use because they see it as a symptom of other deeper psychological problems.

Parents may think that because their son or daughter has a psychological problem, he or she is using substances to alleviate the pain. The mental health problem becomes the focus of their concern. They believe that if the psychological problem is treated, the substance abuse will disappear. Unfortunately, things are not always so simple.

What Problem to Focus On

With teens, it is often hard to distinguish between substance abuse and psychological problems. There is a common debate about what comes first, the depression, for example, or the substance abuse. Did a teen turn to drugs because he was depressed, or did he start using drugs, resulting in the cycle that led to depression? Many teens do try to self-medicate with drugs or alcohol to relieve psychological pain or to try to escape from their problems. There was probably an underlying psychological disorder present before the substance use began. Stopping the use of drugs can exacerbate certain psychological symptoms, causing these teens to seek relief by using drugs again. What happens is that instead of alleviating the psychological problem, these teens develop a drug/alcohol problem too, adding to their difficulties.

The reverse is also true. The use of drugs and alcohol may lead to psychological problems, such as depression. Many substances of abuse are depressants (alcohol being the most widely abused depressant in this country) and can contribute to depressive symptoms. The crash or withdrawal from stimulants can create depressive symptoms as well. And other drugs when abused, while not classified as depressants or stimulants, can create the downward spiral that contributes to feelings of depression. You need to address the social and psychological aspects of your teen's drug abuse. At this point in a teen's use of drugs, the depression may be quite real and not just drug induced. Treating the depression with medication and therapy may be required. But the teen must be drug-free for any form of therapy to be effective. The prescription of anti-depressants will not work as effectively (or may not work at all) if a teen continues to use substances while taking the medication.

The current thinking for many professionals in the mental health field is that, regardless of which came first, both problems must be treated equally. You don't treat the depression, hoping the drug use will go away. You don't treat the drug use without paying attention to psychological problems. Although one problem may have come first, you are now stuck with both of them, and attention to both is essential.

Psychological Problems Seen in Drug Using Teens

The psychological problems seen most frequently in adolescents using drugs and alcohol are depression, anxiety, attention deficit hyperactivity disorder (ADHD), and eating disorders. There are many good books and other resources on adolescents afflicted with these disorders, and their content is beyond the scope of this book. We have included some suggested reading in appendix B. If your teen is exhibiting any signs of these disorders, any psychological workup should explore the possible influence of drugs and alcohol. And conversely, any time a teen is being evaluated for a drug or alcohol problem, questions about psychological problems and family history should be asked.

So how can you tell the difference? The first thing is to think about what your child was like before you found out about his or her drug use. Remembering how your teen functioned prior to using substances may give you a clue as to what came first. If the psychological symptoms have been around for some time, then your teen may be self-medicating with substances. But if the psychological problems started at around the same time as the using, they may be primarily caused by the drug use. No matter what, your child must stop using in order to get relief.

Family Development

Adolescents do not live in isolation. They live in a family structure. Family members witness the changes that adolescents experience and are also affected by them.

Families, too, develop and change over time. Living in a family means that we are affected by one another's development, which in turn, affects the development of the family. When one family member begins to change in a particular way, the rest of the family may have to adjust to that change. Family members begin to change in response to one family member's changes. The scientific term for this process is called homeostasis. If one part is not functioning properly, other parts of an organism (the family, in this case) make adjustments. Homeostasis is an attempt to return the organism to a balanced and functional state.

Family Responses to a Teen's Use/Abuse of Drugs and Alcohol

When a teen's behavior changes because of drug use, families are frequently surprised at this "new person" that now lives in their home. As a teen isolates, becomes more moody, or lashes out in anger at family members, siblings and parents will begin to react, each in their own way. They may either avoid or confront the new behaviors facing them. Interactions and family relationships will change. Time spent together changes, resulting in a family that was moving in a particular direction now taking an unexpected detour.

If a teen's drug use continues and becomes increasingly problematic, the family's development becomes more problematic as well. Not only will the using teen be more isolative and secretive, but frequently families also begin to isolate themselves from the outside world. Other family members hide the difficulties happening at home from extended family or friends. They stop inviting people over to the house. At a time when a family needs support, they may make it more difficult to receive.

Relationship Changes

Family relationships change too. We frequently see shifts in alliances among family members when a teen is using substances. Parents often disagree about how to handle the problem of a teen's drug use. One parent may want to come down harshly and restrict a son or daughter from activities or friends, while the other parent may see it as "just a phase" the teen is going through. Arguments can cause distance between parents when one sides with the teen rather than with the other spouse. In some families, we have seen couples separate (even divorce) over their differences about parenting a drug-using teen.

Other relationships and alliances may change as well when a teen is involved in the use of drugs. Younger siblings may try to emulate an older brother or sister in their rebellious, acting out behavior. They may try to "gang up on" their parents. Sometimes a sibling may try to make up for a brother or sister's troubles by covering for him or her, doing the other's chores or homework. Others may overachieve to draw attention away from the using teen.

Siblings may find themselves getting less attention because of the problems their brother or sister is having, and may begin to resent their parents for the time devoted to helping that sibling. Previously good relationships between parent and children may begin to deteriorate as the feelings of neglect and resentment grow.

These changes can permanently alter the development of a family. Some family relationships will be affected forever. To get healthy family development back on track, healing and reparation must occur.

Renegotiating When Drug Use Stops

If a teen does stop using drugs, the family may be stuck in a new pattern of relating to one another that is not healthy for anyone involved. Often we will hear parents whose teen has stopped using drugs say, "Now I have my child back. This is the person I remember." The problem, which the newly clean teen will often voice, is that now the family has to change. The new direction that the family has taken in adjusting to a drug-using teen may be inappropriate for the changes the teen has made.

Once a teen is clean and sober, a family can renegotiate the limits that have been placed on a teen's behavior. And the teen may have to shift in response to new behaviors from his or her parents. A parent and teen who have become untrusting of one another or defensive and withdrawn, may have to change their views and their behavior in the new situation. A younger sibling who looked up to the using teen will have to reevaluate his or her beliefs if the brother or sister is now drug free. This is especially true if the younger sibling has begun experimenting with drugs. Conversely, siblings who have withdrawn from one another because of different beliefs and behaviors may have to establish a new kind of relationship once the drug use is gone.

Families frequently isolate themselves from extended family or friends because of the problems they have been having with a using teen. When those problems begin to dissipate, a family may have to renegotiate their relationships with people outside the immediate family.

Adolescent development and family development are seriously affected when a teen is using drugs. How much they are affected depends on the degree to which a teen is involved in drug use, what stage of use the teen has reached, and how the family responds. The sooner parents respond, after realizing a son or daughter is using drugs, the less both individual and family development will be negatively affected.

CHAPTER 5

Why Is This
Happening to Us?

WARNING: *IN THIS CHAPTER YOU WILL BE CHALLENGED TO LOOK AT YOURSELF AND YOUR OWN BEHAVIOR.*

Many parents are surprised to discover that their teenager is using drugs or alcohol, especially if substances are being used in a problematic way. Figuring out the hows and whys can be a perplexing and even frightening task. Most parents respond by getting angry, both at their teen and at the world around them. Frequently parents will try to shift the blame on anyone, anything, or anywhere outside the home.

In today's world, there are large numbers of adolescents trying alcohol and other drugs. Trying to find the single cause or reason to explain your teen's drug use is unrealistic, because the reasons are often multitiered. More useful is looking at what factors have contributed to your son or daughter's involvement with drugs and alcohol. Then you can take action and make the necessary changes to turn things around.

The first thing for you to do is take a closer look at what is going on at home, in your own family. And do so without placing blame. When we work with families where a teen is abusing drugs or alcohol, we often find a history of alcoholism or drug dependence in the family. We also find certain typical family dynamics, styles of communication, and patterns of coping with problems. As you take a look at your family, think about your teen's particular makeup and how living in your family affects him or her.

Your next step is to look at the community where you live. There are certain issues in some communities that may contribute to the problem. Taking a closer look at your child's world beyond your family is important.

Sometimes it is hard to pinpoint a cause or reason for the use. However, taking the pulse of your family and examining your family history is usually an important first step in helping your teen through the problem.

Family Issues

Family issues can play a big role in substance abuse problems. We can examine these issues in terms of family history—or genetics—and family dynamics.

Genetics

Research suggests that there is a genetic component to addiction. Adopted children whose biological families have a history of addiction are at risk for developing substance abuse problems as adolescents. Likewise, research on twins also points to a genetic link in addiction (Heath 1995). Studies of different cultures with different biological/ chemical makeups show differences in tolerance for alcohol and in reactions to its effects. For instance, people of Japanese descent have a lower tolerance for alcohol than almost any other culture or ethnic group (Wall and Ehlers 1995). Just as family members can pass down eye color, height, baldness, or a predisposition for diabetes or breast cancer, so too a predisposition to addiction may be passed down from generation to generation (Schuckit 1995). It is not uncommon for a parent of an abusing teen to be an alcoholic or drug addicted, but the substance abuse problem does not have to be with one of the parents. A grandparent, aunt, uncle, or cousin (frequently more than one person in the family) may have or have had a substance abuse problem.

The genogram is a useful tool to help families identify a history of substance abuse/addiction. Basically, a genogram is the equivalent of a therapeutic family tree. Adopted by mental health professionals as a tool for mapping family histories on many issues, it is used by substance abuse professionals to provide a visual picture of the history of an addiction problem in a family.

Once the family history is mapped out, the genogram is helpful in demonstrating patterns in families and in providing a concrete picture of what many family members may already know instinctively. Seeing the patterns makes it more difficult to ignore the existence of such patterns. It gives families an opportunity to reflect, discuss, and in many cases look ahead at what could be in store for younger family members. For instance, in families with a history of breast cancer, knowledge about the pattern of the disease can lead to young women in the family having early and more frequent screening. Similarly, in families with a history of addiction, awareness of family patterns can lead to early detection and prevention of the problem. Teens, equipped with the knowledge that their use of alcohol or drugs puts them at a much higher risk for developing an addiction, may be less likely to use them in the first place. Or at minimum, these teens will be more cautious about using. It is especially helpful when families can openly discuss the negative consequences suffered by a particular family member. This gives teens a concrete example of the consequences of drug abuse.

Figure 1 is Mark and Emily's genogram. Here's what it tells us: Mark's parents, Max and Emma, and their siblings (not pictured) have no addiction problems. Mark, an only child, has a close relationship with his parents. Emily's parents, Phillip and Maria, are divorced. Phillip is an alcoholic. Maria's brother George is an alcoholic. Her alcoholic brother Dino died of cirrhosis of the liver. Emily no longer speaks to her sister, Esther, because she and her husband Edward, have been addicted to amphetamines for years. Their children, Bill and Steven, are also addicted. The family uses together and Esther is overly involved in her son's lives. Mark and Emily, who have a close relationship, have three children, Dino, Douglas, and Suzanna. The eldest, Dino, named after his mother's uncle, is an alcoholic. The youngest, Suzanna, is using amphetamines with her cousins. She hardly speaks to her brother Douglas because he keeps confronting her about her using.

Sounds like a soap opera, doesn't it? No, in fact it is a typical genogram of a family with addiction. The genogram clearly illustrates how addiction runs in families. It shows how addiction may skip a generation and how relationships are affected by addiction. We could surmise that one of Maria's parents was an alcoholic. Even though she herself has never been addicted, she married an alcoholic and is faced with a daughter and grandchildren who are addicts.

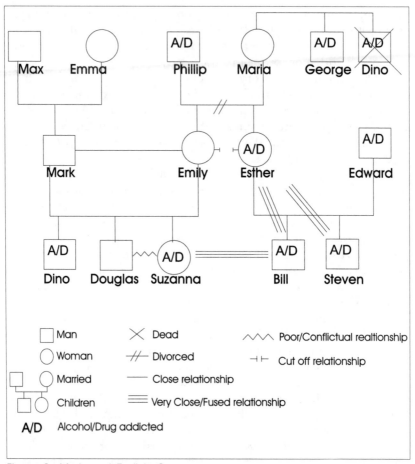

Figure 1: Mark and Emily's Genogram

Emily married Mark because he wasn't an alcoholic, but she is still dealing with addiction through her children. Mark and Emily, after filling out the genogram, have some serious work to do with their children to try to stop the pattern from repeating in future generations.

We've included a blank genogram (figure 2) for you to record your own family history. Fill it out like a family tree, using the key below to identify any addictions in the family and the nature of the relationships between family members. Mark up the genogram in any way that is useful. Include grandparents or grandchildren if it will help you see the big picture. Fill out the genogram with your teen, as well as other family members if you like. It can be a great basis for discussion.

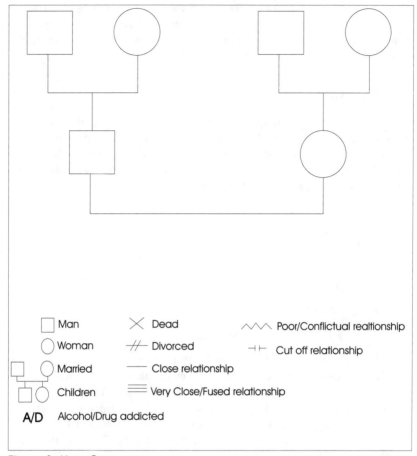

Figure 2: Your Genogram

Family Dynamics

In addition to a genetic component to addiction, certain behavioral patterns in families can be passed down from generation to generation. We frequently see, for example, how children of alcoholics marry an alcoholic or addict. The children may not have an addiction problem themselves, but they have become familiar with life in an alcoholic family. Although they may not like many of the associated patterns of behavior, what is most familiar becomes what is most comfortable.

Even in families without an addiction history, we see similar patterns of relating and coping. There is usually something stressful going on with one or more family members. These stressors have a powerful impact on everyone in the family. Even when people are unaware of the exact problems, they are affected. Remember, the problems of one family member affect everyone in the family.

Family Roles

When there is a major problem or crisis in a family, everyone tries to find the best way they can to cope with the situation. People will do and say things they ordinarily would never consider. They fall into certain roles in the family as a way to cope with the problems. Typical roles seen in families in crisis are

- user, or victim

- enabler

- hero

- scapegoat

- lost child

- mascot (Wegscheider-Cruse 1989)

The *user* or victim is the family member that initially causes the family distress. Users are often in denial about their problematic behavior. They may feel self-righteous and try to justify their behavior to the family. They frequently blame other family members for their problems and may be angry or aggressive toward others.

The *enabler* assumes primary responsibility for shielding the substance user from the harmful consequences of his or her behavior. Often the enabler is the spouse of a using person, but with drug-abusing teens, the enabler is generally a parent (or sometimes a grandparent). The enabler becomes overly controlling and responsible, then feels like the victim who suffers the most.

The *hero* provides the family with a feeling of self-worth. The hero is generally independent and successful in the outside world. The hero is usually helpful to the family, taking on a caretaker role.

The *scapegoat* provides distraction. The scapegoat draws attention away from the real problem, creating other problems for the family to focus on. The scapegoat may too become a substance abuser or act out in other destructive ways.

The *lost child* offers relief to the family by not becoming a problem to focus on. The lost child will isolate and withdraw from the rest of the family and does not have to be noticed at all, positively or negatively. The lost child isn't connected to other family members.

The *mascot* provides fun and humor for the family. The mascot is usually cute, charming, and fun to be around. He or she is not taken seriously by anyone but likes to be the center of attention.

Coping Behaviors

Frequently the behaviors and roles in families dealing with addiction can be destructive, both to the individuals and to the rest of the family. Families don't start out trying to be unhealthy. Everyone is just trying to manage the best they can. When you've grown up in a family with harmful patterns, you're likely to carry those patterns into the family you create as an adult. It's what you know. The patterns are repeated until the family recognizes them and decides to find new ways of coping.

The first behavior that family members share is denial. The family acts like they're walking around in a trance, unaware of what is right before their eyes. An analogy used in drug treatment programs is that in these families it is as if there is "an elephant in the living room." There is a huge problem getting in the family's way. It takes up more and more space. The family has to walk around it and clean up after it, but no one does anything about it. No one talks about it. The family just hopes it will go away. Instead, everyone's denial just maintains the problem.

Not only do we see denial of the problem, but there is also a denial of individual family members' needs or feelings. Needs go underground. It becomes unacceptable to have needs because the family already feels drained of energy to deal with any more problems. Most feelings are not allowed expression and can't be dealt with openly or honestly. If no one is acknowledging that there is a problem, then you can't say you're afraid of it, or that you are angry and resentful, or embarrassed. As the denial continues, family members may not even be able to identify what they are feeling, let alone express those feelings to other family members.

Common feelings that arise in these families are guilt, shame, resentment, and insecurity. Parents will feel guilty for a teen's abuse issues. They may feel they have gone wrong in raising an addicted child. If a parent is using, other family members often feel responsible. They believe that something about them or their behavior is causing the person to use. Shame will cause family members to withdraw from social contacts and be afraid to seek help. Resentments may build, and family members may behave disrespectfully toward each other. The family begins to feel they'd be better off if the using person just went away. Insecurity occurs because living with an addict creates an unpredictable environment at home. The family just doesn't know how the addict is going to act.

These families tend to develop rigid rules for how family members can behave. There is usually so much chaos that sticking to a very narrow way of behaving keeps the family together. Family members commonly exhibit black-and-white thinking or all-or-nothing thinking. There is an intolerance of others' opinions and people aren't allowed to make mistakes. Individuals get stuck in a particular role and find it hard to be anything else in the family. As a result, these families lack joy or spontaneity. They may find it hard to express humor. Children frequently misbehave or break the rules when they're away from home because they feel so restricted at home. They can't take risks in the family, so they find ways to do so on the outside.

We also often see triangulation. That's when parents use the kids to communicate with each other. As a result, the alliance between the parents is broken. When parents are less connected, it can lead to unnatural alliances between family members. A parent may lean on one of the children as a companion or confidante. That parent and child may almost gang up against the other parent. The most extreme example of these unnatural alliances is when a lack of generational boundaries leads to incest. Unfortunately, when some adults are troubled, and alcohol or other drugs are used, they may become disinhibited and engage in this kind of destructive behavior that affects all involved.

Cross-generational alliances also happen in families with divorced parents. Many teens feel this alliance with one parent as a burden. Although there are some rewards—extra attention, more power in the family, or getting away with things they otherwise wouldn't—the alliance is usually more than a teen can handle.

Family members also cope by keeping secrets about problems and behaviors from other family members. Secrets can be between spouses, siblings, or a parent and child. They fear what another family member might say or do. It's difficult to face problems directly with honesty and trust. A parent may be having an affair, a divorce may be pending, there may be a family illness, or a family member may be in some kind of trouble: each of these problems can become secrets to hide from other family members. We'll frequently see one parent keeping a teen's alcohol or drug use from the other parent. Secrets such as this are very destructive to the family unit.

Boundary Problems

Another way of looking at family dynamics is to examine how family members handle boundaries. Boundaries are important for healthy individuals and families. In families with addiction or other stressors, boundaries are often absent, or conversely, they may be too rigid.

Individual boundaries: When people have no boundaries, they have no personal space or time. They aren't able to turn down requests and it's hard for them to make decisions. They don't feel valued. This can lead to low self-esteem. Family members with weak individual boundaries become overly concerned with other family members' problems, to the point where the problems feel like their own. Teens who experience this with their parents will have a harder time separating. They can become overly attached to a parent. Sometimes they have to break away in more extreme ways, by using alcohol or drugs.

Conversely, if boundaries are too rigid, then family members can't share with one another. There is no give and take and everyone feels isolated. A teen may feel that the only way to get emotional closeness is to go outside of the family. At a time when teens are turning to friends more anyway, there is no backup at home. There's no one with whom the teen can share his or her difficulties.

Generational boundaries: When generational boundaries are crossed, the lines of authority in the family are unclear. Rules and consequences are vague, leading to inconsistency and unpredictability. Children may have an inordinate amount of power. Teens can feel like they are the ones in charge. This, too, is when unnatural alliances between generations are formed. Children are asked to fill emotional or physical needs the parents can't fulfill for each other.

When generational boundaries are too rigid, parents can't express how they feel to their kids. Parents are physically and emotionally absent, making it difficult for them to show love to the kids, or even each other. They can't empathize with their kids. They don't seem to care. The rules set up by the parents are inflexible and unyielding. Teens in this situation often turn to substances for comfort.

Family boundaries: When families don't have good boundaries, people flow in and out. There is no one in charge, so there are few limits or rules. Instead, there is chaos. There doesn't seem to be any family unity; the family feels fragmented. Children experience this as a family with no solid core. They frequently go outside of the family to find the stability they need. Teens will turn to friends and their friends' families. Or they can turn to drugs.

When family boundaries are too rigid, the family isolates itself from the outside world. There's an attitude of "don't air your dirty laundry in public." Friends aren't invited over. Families think they have to solve all their problems themselves and won't reach out for help. When this happens, and a teen is using alcohol or drugs, the problem usually gets very serious and out of control before anyone on the outside notices. Teens may end up in jail or the emergency room before they can get the help they need.

If you recognize any of these patterns or behaviors in your family, don't despair. This is not the time for shame, guilt, or resentment. Indulging in those feelings will only lead to a continuation of unhealthy patterns. It is important to be able to identify these behavior patterns. Until you are aware of these patterns, you will stay in the trance and feel immobilized. Recognizing the problems is the first step to making healthy changes. This is a good thing. It's an opportunity to begin the process of healing.

Parental Substance Use

As you figure out what is happening with your child, it is important to examine your own use of drugs and alcohol. Your drinking or drug use has an impact on your teen. Your child will be influenced by your behavior, however minimal or severe your use is. If there is a family history of addiction, your use of substances deserves a great deal of scrutiny.

If you answer "yes" to any of the following questions, you may have a substance abuse problem.

- Has drinking or using drugs stopped being fun?

- Do you drink or use drugs alone?

- Is it hard for you to imagine a life without alcohol or drugs?

- Do you find that your friends are determined by their drinking or drug use?

- Do you drink or use drugs to avoid dealing with your problems?

- Do you drink or use drugs to enhance or change your feelings?

- Have you ever failed to keep promises about cutting down or controlling your drinking or drug use?

- Do you have difficulty remembering what you said or did after drinking or using drugs?

- When you are almost out of liquor or drugs, do you feel anxious or worried? Is getting more what occupies your mind?

- Do you plan your life around your drinking or drug use?

- Have friends/family ever complained that your drinking or drug use is damaging your relationship with them?

- Do you continue to drink or use drugs in spite of negative consequences?

The questions above are used in treatment programs and in twelve-step programs (like Alcoholics Anonymous) to help diagnose abuse or addiction. People with positive responses to two or more of these questions are given recommendations for treatment. At twelve-step meetings, they are told they are in the right place.

Even if there is no family history, or you believe you are not abusing or addicted to any substance, your patterns of use and reasons for drinking or using drugs should be examined. Your teen may have learned coping strategies from you that include the use of substances. Your child may see drug use or drinking as a necessary part of adulthood. Ask yourself a few pertinent questions.

- Is your drinking or use of drugs a ritual, occurring at the same times or places on a routine basis?

- Do you drink or use drugs to feel comfortable socially?

- Is alcohol a part of most social or family gatherings?

- Do you drink or use drugs to relax after a day at work?

- Do you consider drinking or using drugs a reward for a hard day's work?

- Do you drink or use drugs when you are angry or sad, as a way to forget or to feel less intensely?

If you answered "yes" to any of these questions, your use may not be a problem but perhaps it is a habit. This does not necessarily mean it is a bad habit, but it is something that is commonplace in your life. By example, you communicate the acceptance of this habit to your children. You may be telling them through your actions that to have fun with friends means you drink, that to relax means you take a substance, and that alcohol or drugs are a reward or prize and a necessary part of celebration. As your kids move into adolescence and want to try out adult behaviors, using drugs and alcohol may seem a natural thing to do.

We are not saying that you should never use substances. That is a decision for you to make for yourself. You may have determined that your use is not problematic, or you may have decided that you are not ready or willing to change your drinking or using behavior at this time. Your use of substances is up to you. If your teen is abusing or addicted, though, we do recommend that you keep drugs or alcohol out of the home and never use or drink in your teen's presence. Teens who are seriously trying to abstain from using drugs and alcohol are advised to avoid people and places where drugs and alcohol are found. Their struggle is difficult enough without being confronted by the use of substances right in their own home. Home should be a safe haven from the world of drugs and alcohol.

Many parents ask us if they can teach their kids how to drink responsibly. Although we believe adults can drink responsibly, there is no such thing for children. Drinking is illegal for teens, it is dangerous for their healthy development, and they are not mature enough to make the kind of informed choices that you make. Allowing teens to drink or use drugs in your home rather than out on the street or in a car may seem like teaching responsible use. You may think, "Well, at least I know they are safe." But all you're doing is allowing them to use and communicating that using is okay. Some parents even report that they have used drugs with their children to teach them how to use responsibly. We disagree with this approach. We believe it is condoning a behavior and promoting a lifestyle that is unhealthy for a minor.

Please remember that your teen is in the process of separating from you. Part of separating is about pushing the limits, going beyond what parents say is okay. If you communicate that drinking or drug use is okay, even if only under certain conditions, your teen may have to push the limits to even further extremes for separation to occur. We know very few teens who actually enjoy the taste of alcohol and drink to savor the flavor in a glass of wine. Most teens drink to get drunk, which can lead to horrible consequences.

Your attitude about your teen's drug and alcohol use does have an effect on whether or not your teen drinks or uses substances. The SAMHSA study on teen use of alcohol and drugs found that parental attitudes matter. When asked if their "parents would strongly disapprove if they tried marijuana once or twice," only 7.1 percent of teens ages twelve to seventeen who answered "yes" had used an illicit drug in the past month. But 31.2 percent of teens who answered "no" (their parents would not strongly disapprove), reported that they had used an illicit drug in the past month (SAMHSA 2001). What you think and what you condone does matter!

Beyond Your Family

Now that we have encouraged you to take a close look at your family, including family genetics, modeling of coping strategies, and family dynamics, let's also look at the community in which you live. Again, the reason is not to place blame. Too often parents will try to blame the school, or their child's friends, or even the music their son/daughter listens to all the time.

Schools do their best to teach about the dangers of drugs and alcohol, but they can only do so much. As for your child's friends, they are probably not to blame, either. In fact, it may be your child who has started a friend on drugs. And it isn't the music alone that has caused the problems your teen is facing. Today's adolescents are living in a very different world than we've ever seen before. The amount of drugs available, the violence in schools and on the streets, and the tragedies in our larger community have all placed a difficult burden on teens and their parents. An old African saying, " It takes a village to raise a child," reminds us that families used to be able to rely on the community to help with child rearing. For most of us, this is no longer the norm. Parents are on their own and expected to know all and do all for their kids. As our kids move into adolescence, many of us no longer know their teachers. We often don't know the parents of our kids' friends.

What we have found is that teens often find themselves in situations that feel beyond their control. Your child, in the process of forming an identity, has made choices about his or her interests, how to spend free time, and whom to befriend. Although the ideal for healthy development is to move in and out of various interests or groups of friends, many teens can get stuck and end up feeling trapped. They may find themselves using drugs regularly and not know what to do about it. They may not have the skills to stand up for themselves. They may not have the confidence to stand out from the crowd. Although they may know that a group of friends is not good for them, they may not know how to extricate themselves. They might realize that their choices have limited their possibilities but still not know what to do about it.

This is when it is important for you, as a parent, to intervene. This is when turning to your community and any available resources must begin. First, you should try to help your son or daughter determine what is best for them and find ways to make that happen. How can they reinvent themselves? Some teens can do this by joining up with a different set of teens through a youth group or club. They can find new interests or rediscover old interests that they have dropped. They can decide to attend summer school and catch up on missed coursework. You can also elicit the help of teachers, school counselors, a therapist, or a pastor. Ultimately, your son or daughter has to make their world work for them, but you can help by making suggestions and offering some choices for how to negotiate a new path.

Sometimes, redirecting teens in this way can help them get out of a dead-end situation. But some teens cannot reinvent themselves with such simple solutions. They feel too stuck or trapped. Some parents have tried to help their children by changing schools. Other parents have moved to a new part of town or even to an entirely new community in order to give their teens a chance to make a fresh start. This can be very effective for some teens, especially when families live in neighborhoods that are infested with drugs. If you decide to make such a move, your teen could experience a sense of relief that you have stepped in and helped him or her out of what felt like an impossible situation.

Unfortunately, this kind of change does not work for everyone. We have seen families move to a new neighborhood only to find that their child is still using drugs. Their teen may have found a similar group of friends at the new school or at least found someone to buy drugs from. Sometimes it feels like the problem just follows the child wherever the child goes. In such cases, the teen may be in too deep, and his or her drug use is not due to environmental factors at all. The problem is now an addiction and the teen will struggle with it wherever the family goes—at least until he or she gets some help.

Determine the Reasons

No matter what stage of use your teen is in, it's helpful to determine what the use is about. For many teens, this struggle is a result of more than one factor. Perhaps there is a family history. Perhaps your family is immersed in destructive patterns. Perhaps your child has had psychological problems for a long while. Perhaps your teen did get involved with the wrong crowd, or you live in an area with a lot of drug and alcohol use. Maybe this is just the twenty-first century when drugs and alcohol are readily available to adolescents and use among teens is on the rise.

You need to figure out where or how this all began so that you can decide what to do about it. Determine what stage of use your teen is in. Your response and the help you seek will depend on where your child falls on the continuum of substance use. Utilize a therapist with expertise in substance abuse or get an evaluation from a drug treatment center to help you determine your child's level of use. You will come up with the best approach for your teen and family, depending on that assessment. After identifying family patterns that have been unhealthy for you or other family members, you can seek help from a mental health professional with expertise in family therapy to help you change those patterns. And after assessing the risks of your child remaining in his or her current environment, talk to school personnel and others in your community who will support you in making any necessary changes. Whatever you do, be sure to get support from family, friends, and professionals to help you with an assessment and to help you determine what your next steps are.

Letting Go

The bottom line is that your teen is involved in using drugs or alcohol. We want to caution you that there is a danger in getting too attached to the reasons and causes for your teen's use. Although it's helpful to determine the root causes of the problem, you need to stay focused on your goal, which is to get the help your teen needs. Staying focused on the reasons can lead to blame, and blaming anyone or anything won't fix the problem. You will just get stuck in a vicious cycle of anger, blame, and remorse. You and your teen are where you are, and it's time to begin a process of letting go. Just figure out what you can about the situation and move on.

Letting go means you can't go backward and fix the past. You can't control everyone and everything in your teen's life. Trying to change the past or change other people is futile. You need to determine what you can do and let go of what you can't control.

It may seem contradictory to be told to let go and give up control when the child you love is so out of control. We aren't saying to give up. Quite the contrary. You have a long road ahead of you in turning things around. What we are saying is that change begins from within. Begin to change those things that you can. Start with how you can approach your teen and the situation differently. Make your own changes at the same time you try to turn things around for your child. Take an especially close look at those things you have found in your family that need work. Start there. It's a very good place to begin.

CHAPTER 6

What Doesn't Work

This chapter focuses on parental behaviors that are guaranteed to fail if your child has a substance abuse problem. You may already have fallen into some bad habits—and this chapter will help you examine what you may be doing wrong. In chapter 7, we will go on to discuss some ways to improve your approach to your teen's problems. But for now, please go back to chapter 1 and review the items you've checked in group D of the Parent's Awareness Checklist. Then return to this chapter.

Parents try to raise their children as well as they can. Unfortunately, sometimes it seems that the only options parents have are among different choices of what can go wrong. What's a parent to do? Perhaps the first step is to eliminate those choices that are known to be unproductive, that are guaranteed to *not* bring about the positive results you want to achieve.

Codependency

Don't be a codependent! Don't be an enabler! That's all the professionals ever talk about. What are they talking about? What do they really mean?

Adherents of Alcoholic's Anonymous's disease model of addiction classify codependence as another addictive disease. Codependents are people whose lives have become unmanageable as a result of living with an alcoholic or drug addict. Another way of looking at the situation was suggested by *Codependent No More* author Melody Beattie (1996). She believed that a codependent person was someone who has let another person's behavior affect him/her and who is obsessed with trying to control that person's behavior. Codependency may also involve a loss of your sense of inner reality, an inability to trust your own feelings, and an inability to act spontaneously.

Some characteristics of codependency include

- a feeling of low self-worth (or low self-esteem)
- difficulty in identifying and expressing feelings
- caretaking of others, at expense to self
- difficulty in making decisions
- a tendency to try to control others by manipulation
- perfectionism, too many expectations of self and others
- difficulty in adjusting to change
- an inability to set boundaries
- rigidity, feeling stuck in an attitude
- obsessive worrying
- a general feeling of powerlessness
- a tendency to try to rescue or fix others

Instead of doing an old-fashioned square dance, codependents do the dysfunctional triangle dance. The following diagram is based on the work of Stephen B. Karpman, and is known as the Karpman Drama Triangle (1968).

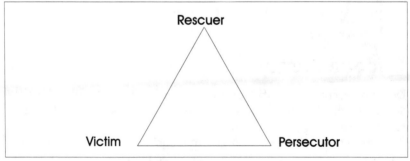

Figure 3: Karpman Drama Triangle

The dance begins with the codependent person trying to rescue someone. For example, the rescuer may make excuses or cover up for a drug-abusing teen who has failed to take responsibility for him- or herself. After the rescue, the codependent person feels used and sorry for him- or herself. In fact, the former rescuer now feels victimized and unappreciated. The last step in the dance is to blame the other person for these feelings, and to persecute this person by getting angry and yelling, or worse, cutting them off by withdrawing.

Enabling grows out of the same healthy instincts that lead parents to protect their young. Parents will go to great lengths to nurture that precious new life. It's very hard to stop that process, even when it becomes obvious that the enabling behavior is now destructive to growth, even when it may actually be contributing to your drug-addicted teen's potentially lethal continued use.

Basically, enabling behavior consists of offering the wrong kind of help. It's the kind of "help" that prevents a teen from experiencing the natural consequences of his or her bad decisions. In an attempt to protect the teen, the enabler allows, and sometimes even encourages, the teen to continue drinking or doing drugs.

Behavioral Strategies That Don't Work

Here are some of the specific behaviors that may be contributing to your becoming an enabling, codependent parent. See how many of them seem familiar to you, or hit close to home.

Denial. In this context, *denial* means ignoring the obvious signs of drug or alcohol abuse in your child. Professionals like to call denial "the river in Egypt," partly because it's been around forever. No parent wants to acknowledge that their teen is abusing drugs or alcohol. Maybe parents go into denial because they feel ashamed or embarrassed. Sometimes parents believe that admitting that their child has a drug problem is also a tacit admission of their failure as a parent. Sometimes denial can be a convenient delaying device. It allows parents to take some time when they feel overwhelmed by the reality of the teen's substance abuse. Acknowledging the problem would mean that they would have to do something about it.

Example: "Jamal doesn't have a drug problem. He's just going through a phase."

Minimizing. This is the concept of making a molehill out of a mountain of evidence. When parents don't admit to the severity of the problem, they have an excuse to avoid having to deal with it. Unfortunately, they often wait until the problem is out of control.

Example: "It's not so bad, Todd only comes home drunk sometimes. At least he's not doing drugs."

Colluding. In legal terms, this is called being an accessory before or after the fact. You're guilty of colluding when you know that your teen's behavior is wrong, but you help him or her anyway.

Example: "Okay, I'll buy a keg for your birthday party. But keep it out of sight in the backyard."

Covering up. This is a form of deception that may mean lying to a spouse or an employer about your child's behavior. Sometimes it means making excuses to friends and family. At worst, it involves lying to people who are trying to help, such as probation officers.

Example: "I'm not going to tell your P.O. about you missing curfew. I don't want to get you into more trouble. But you'd better shape up, young man."

Overprotecting. This means not allowing your teen to face the consequences of his or her actions. Parents want to protect their children from the harsh realities of life. Sometimes, though, the best thing for your child is to allow him or her to learn from painful experience.

Example: "We have to take care of Tiffany and keep her safe. She's our precious little girl."

Rescuing. When you rescue your teen by continually bailing him or her out of trouble, you're teaching your child that he or she does not have to be responsible. In the long run, if teens are treated this way, they end up being unprepared to take care of themselves and handle life on their own.

Example: "I had to put up Jeremy's bail. I didn't want him to spend the night in jail with those criminals."

Self-blaming. Beating yourself up doesn't help anything, either. In your heart, you know that you're not responsible for your child's drug abuse. At worst, blaming yourself gives your teen another way to avoid taking responsibility for his or her own behavior.

Example: "If only we had gotten Sarah some help sooner, it wouldn't have come to this."

Blaming others. The problem is always somebody else's fault. Your teen is never to blame or responsible for what's going wrong. Again, though it's tempting to look for external causes, doing so will only make matters worse.

Example: "You're never home. That's why James has no role models except for those drug dealers on the street."

Rationalizing. You may find yourself arguing that a bad situation is really not so bad. Pretending that your drug-abusing teen is not abusing drugs, however, will not make him or her quit abusing drugs. The bad situation will not go away.

Example: "I tried marijuana and psychedelic drugs when I was a teen too, and I turned out fine."

Avoidance. Many parents avoid confronting their teen's behavior because they don't want to start an argument, or don't want the teen to think they distrust him or her. And sometimes they simply just don't want to know the truth.

Example: "I don't want to know what time Ted came home last night. I'm just glad that he's home safe and sound."

Bargaining. This is a desperate attempt by parents to try to get a handle on an out-of-control teen. Rather than take charge by setting limits, they try to bribe the teen into reasonable behavior.

Example: "Here's the deal. If you stop smoking marijuana, I'll buy you that new CD player."

Befriending. If you're lucky, you can develop a friendship with your kids once they've grown up, left the house, and established independent lives. However, while your children are growing up, they need you to be an adult, a parent who is a good role model and sets appropriate boundaries rather than trying to be "hip" or "with it."

Codependents frequently feel like, "If you can't beat 'em, join 'em." But again, this can look like you're condoning the behavior and only contribute to ongoing use.

Example: "Trish, let's go shopping at the mall. Then maybe we can grab some lunch and share a glass of wine together."

Shaming. Shaming is certainly one of the most harmful practices that parents can engage in. It makes your child feel small, bad, and wrong. Usually a teen will resort to more drinking and drug use to obliterate those feelings.

Example: "You're drug use has embarrassed our entire family, I'm ashamed to have you for a son."

Doing nothing. A laissez-faire attitude may sometimes be desirable as a foreign policy for the government, but it's not helpful in a home with a drinking or drug-abusing teen. The more parents do nothing, the longer it will take for the teen to turn his or her life around.

Example: "I know it looks like Cindy is using ecstasy and going to raves. But I'm afraid if we tell her not to, she'll just start lying to us."

Communication Styles That Don't Work

It's not simply your behavioral strategies that may be problematic. The way that you communicate with your teen may cause problems as well.

Confronting. This communication style is a little tricky. There's nothing wrong with confrontation in general, but it really matters how and when it's done. Too much confrontation too soon is apt to backfire. If, for example, you ground your son for a month after discovering him sneaking a cigarette, you may not get the compliance you had hoped for. Blasting your kid for a relatively minor infraction may just lead to rebellion and secrecy.

On the other hand, too little confrontation too late will do no good at all. After your daughter comes home drunk for the third time, she may shrug off a mild lecture and the loss of TV privileges for a week.

And it's not just the degree of confrontation, it's the timing that's crucial too. The first rule is to *never* confront your teen when he or she is high on alcohol or drugs. Unless your teen is sober at the time of confrontation, you're just wasting your time. In reality, you're talking to the drug, not to the teen. The most likely result will be a belligerent, angry exchange that will lead to more conflict, not a useful resolution. And don't confront your teen when you are angry. That's a sure way to get nowhere.

Lecturing. There's no better way to turn off the reception antennae in your teen's head than for you to start lecturing. An example of a potential lecture is an attempt at communication that begins with the words, "I want you to listen to me, young lady . . ." or "When I was your age . . ." This is inevitably doomed to failure. After the first few words, the automatic tune-out mechanism kicks in and your teen is gone.

Nagging. This is like playing a broken record over and over and over. Sure, you want your teen to stop drinking and doing drugs. Sure, maybe he's got a terrible memory and has forgotten what you said yesterday. Sure, maybe she just didn't hear you. Sure, maybe all your teen needs is just one more reminder. Sure.

Ridicule. Teens have very fragile self-esteem and are excruciatingly sensitive to negative comments. They may not show it, but comments like "You look like something the cat dragged in . . ." or "You don't need a second helping of dessert, you're heavy enough already" can be devastating. Many teens with a low self-image use drugs as a way to feel better. Your contribution to their poor self-esteem can't help. Another form of ridicule is the use of sarcasm. For example, if your teen son sleeps in on a Saturday morning and comes to the kitchen at 10:00 A.M., don't greet him with, "Good morning . . . or is it afternoon?"

Overreacting. If there's one thing kids are experts at, it's knowing how to push your buttons. Sometimes all they need to do is just keep silent and roll their eyes, or walk into the house and deliberately drop their coat on the living room floor. Whatever it takes to make you go ballistic, that's exactly what they'll do. And the worst thing that you can do is to give them the satisfaction of your out-of-control response. They want you to lose control so the focus can shift to you and your problems. That way their own out-of-control behavior is less evident.

An example of an overreaction on your part would be: "That's it! Wipe that smirk off your face. You're grounded for a month . . . without TV."

Global labeling. Sometimes when you're overreacting to your teen's behavior, you might be tempted to make sweeping negative judgments. These are the kind of statements that tend to stigmatize your teen and turn them into a one-dimensional nonperson. An example would be, "You never could do anything right from the time you were born. You'll always be a loser." Or this one: "There you go, smoking marijuana again. You're nothing but a worthless pothead."

Accusations. One sure way of starting a negative communication loop is to make an accusation. And by the way, it doesn't matter if you're right or wrong. It's the very act of making an accusation that creates the problem. Here's an example: "You're the one who has been sneaking into my liquor cabinet. And don't lie to me about it." Saying this will put your child on the defensive, and will result in a negative and unproductive interaction.

Guilt-tripping. Here's an example: "Don't you see how much you're hurting me?" Or "Is this how you pay us back after all we've done for you?"

Please remember, your teen's drug or alcohol abuse problems are not about you or your feelings. This behavior on the part of teens is a desperate attempt to make themselves feel better. Trying to make them feel guilty will only end up making them feel worse, and usually leads to increased drinking or drug use.

Belittling. Saying things to your teen that make him or her feel small or unappreciated is another way to erode your teen's fragile self-esteem. Belittling your son's friends for example, by saying something like "All your friends are a bunch of losers," will tend only to put him on the defensive. And probably will just strengthen his connection to the group as well.

Self-blaming. These are the kind of statements that take the focus off the teen and reinforce the idea that she or he is not responsible for what happens. An example would be, "It's all my fault. I should have never let you go to Sally's party without a chaperone."

Defending. This kind of communication style is another way of allowing your teen to abdicate responsibility for his or her behavior: for example, "It's the whole school system that's messed up. My Joey is being singled out and treated unfairly." Your child is never wrong. Never at fault. It's always something external that's to blame for the problems your teen is having.

Condemnation. A teen's natural response to feeling condemned by his parents is resentment and anger. Teens generally get defensive and lash out, attacking in return. Here's an example: Parent: "If you keep on smoking pot like that you'll end up a worthless bum." Teen: "Oh yeah. You're not such a great success yourself. Besides, you drink like a fish."

Judging. Being judgmental is another good way to alienate your child, and drive him or her further into drug use. When a teen keeps hearing judgmental statements, it just makes him or her want to shut out the outside world all the more. An example of a judging statement is, "You're always messing up. You're just no good, and you never will be."

Joking. Humor is great when it's used to defuse a tense situation or to ease a painful moment. It's not so great when used to avoid facing the reality of substance abuse: "Oh, here's Charlie. He's practicing his Dean Martin routine."

Violence

No chapter on what *doesn't* work would be complete without discussing the possibility of violence, which can take physical, emotional, or verbal forms.

Tolerating violence. Do not tolerate violence from a substance-abusing teen. Set clear limits with consequences for a teen's verbal or emotionally violent behavior. If your child becomes physically violent, call the police.

Threatening violence. On the other hand, threatening your teen with violence doesn't work, either. The threat of violence, no matter who it comes from, creates an environment of fear. This can increase the likelihood of drinking or drug abuse as a coping mechanism.

Child abuse. Carl Anderson, Ph.D., and his colleagues at McLean Hospital in Belmont, Massachusetts conducted a five-year study on the link between child physical and sexual abuse and later drug and alcohol abuse (Anderson et al. 2002). Researchers examined thirty-two subjects, fifteen with a history of childhood abuse and seventeen non-abused controls. They discovered that repeated abuse may lead to reduced blood flow to and impaired development of the cerebellar vermis. This is the area of the brain that regulates dopamine, a brain chemical often associated with drug and alcohol abuse. The article concludes that damage to the cerebellar vermis can lead to irritability and that people with such damage may be more likely to use drugs or alcohol and seek external means, to ease the irritability. If you know that your child was abused in the past, you may want to take this into consideration when evaluating treatment options.

If you want to find the most effective ways to deal with your drug-using teen, you first must be aware of what not to do. Too often, parents act on instinct, or copy what their own parents did that worked for them. Or, they may rely on what worked for an older sibling, a person very different from the teen they're dealing with now. That's what this chapter was all about. The next chapter will tell you about all of those behaviors that can begin to help to turn your teen around.

CHAPTER 7

What Does Work

Deciding how to respond to your teen's use of drugs and alcohol should be based on where your teen falls on the continuum of use. The stage your teen is in should determine your response strategy. A teen in the abuse stage is in a very different predicament than a teen who has just started experimenting with substances within the past three months. It just makes sense to treat the situations differently.

Principles of Good Parenting

Having said that, there are certain responses that seem to work across the board. No matter what stage of use your teen is in, you should rely on a few basic principles of parenting. First and foremost, you need to separate your teen from the problem. If your teen is just starting out in his or her experimentation, it doesn't mean he or she is an immoral, stupid, or bad person. Your teen is just doing what over 80 percent of teens in this country are also doing. This doesn't make it right, or okay, but it probably says more about the world we live in today than about your teen's character. Even if you discover that your teen is much further along the continuum of use, perhaps addicted, it is important to respond to the addiction as an affliction, a problem to be dealt with. Your child is not the addiction! And as you would with any problem your child has, focus on how to make the situation better and support him or her in any way you can.

Your teen may seem like a very different person. Sometimes parents find it difficult to remember what they still love about their teen. Your child's positive personality traits and endearing qualities are hidden in a chemical fog. Keep this in mind. Your child is still the wonderful person you raised. That person has just temporarily disappeared.

Secondly, it is essential to remain calm and in control. Crises often make us "lose it" to the point where we do and say things we later regret. Find ways to keep yourself relaxed and focused on what you want to accomplish. Figure out what you are going to say to your teen before you get into a confrontation. If you find yourself too upset to interact in a civil manner at a given moment, stop and come back to it when you've calmed down. Drug-using teens behave in a very irrational manner. And one irrational person in a discussion is enough. Also, get the support you need from your spouse or significant other, as well as from family and friends. Ask them for help, or seek advice from professionals in the field to develop the best strategy to help your teen. Acknowledge your feelings, but avoid letting your emotions dictate your actions. And try to remember that a crisis can be an opportunity for growth.

Thirdly, it is imperative that parents unite in whatever strategy they are using to help their child. Whether married or divorced, parents often have different ideas on how to approach a teen's drug problem. Resolve your differences before talking with your son or daughter. You can approach your teen separately, but the message must be the same. Work with a professional who is experienced in family therapy and addiction if necessary, and then come together with a solid plan. We know this can be very difficult for many parents, especially those who are divorced. You may not agree on any other issue, or think you have anything in common anymore, but you still share parenting and always will. You must find a way to put your differences aside for the sake of your child.

Respond to Teens in the Early Stages

The focus in this chapter will be on what works for teens in the earlier stages of use. The chapter is designed to help you respond to teen behaviors that are described in group A of the Parent's Awareness Checklist (see chapter 1). If you can catch the problem early, before your teen's use of drugs and alcohol becomes a real problem, you will be able to resolve it more quickly and easily. The deeper your child gets into using drugs and alcohol, the more time, energy, and patience you will need. And the situation will call for more restrictive treatment and drastic measures on your part.

Drug treatment programs that are most successful with teens have similar key elements. These elements mirror the characteristics we find in healthy families. Staffs working in adolescent drug treatment centers are quick to acknowledge that they are not only therapists for these teens but surrogate parents. Other teens who are in treatment serve as surrogate siblings. In fact, some programs actually refer to the group or community as "the family."

Teens in the experimental or even the regular use stage of chemical use may not need a drug treatment program. Instead, it is important to provide all the elements of a good drug treatment program right in your own home. What is important for these teens is a stable, well-functioning home environment. If you can institute these key elements at home while your teen is in the early stages of use, you may be able to avoid the need for a drug treatment program later on. Here's what works in drug treatment programs and in healthy family environments:

- Structure and lots of it. When there is free, unstructured time, it is closely monitored

- Strong adult figures who serve as role models, guides, and gentle disciplinarians

- A positive, warm, and loving atmosphere

- Clear and consistent rules and limits

- Clear and consistent rewards and consequences

- An accepting environment, where adults and teens can learn from their mistakes

- Clear and frequent communication channels between adults and teens

- A sense of unity and shared goals

- High regard for honesty, truth, and being yourself

- Healthy rituals

- Designated responsibilities for each person

- Knowledge about adolescent development and teen substance abuse

- Ability to have fun and to use humor

Provide Structure

Teens thrive in structured environments. They feel safe and secure when the boundaries and family roles are clear. To really succeed, they need structure to gain an understanding of how things work in their world. Scheduled time, rules and limits, consequences, and the organization of the family are all part of a structured environment. When teens have a full schedule of activities, there is less idle time, which means less boredom and less time to spend getting high. Teens using drugs often explain that they use because there is nothing for them to do and they are bored. Structured activities can mean adult contact, which provides supervision and guidance along the way. It also means that the teen is involved in something of interest or an activity that furthers academic, social, or extracurricular goals.

Luckily, teens have built-in structure when they are attending school. They are surrounded by adults who guide and monitor their activities. Their time is focused on directed pursuits and accounted for from morning until afternoon. But most school days end by mid-afternoon. And many parents are working and unavailable during after-school hours. If your teen is going to avoid using drugs during these hours, he or she must have something positive to do. Get your teen involved in a sport, a musical instrument, a club, or a job—something! Set up a schedule where your teen has something to do each day after school. The activity must be one that can be verified. Even if it's just a list of chores to do, you should be able to check it out, having proof that it has been accomplished.

Many teens will protest and complain that they have too much homework to busy themselves with these activities. Our experience is that this is usually a smokescreen to cover the fact that they'd rather just have free time and be able to goof off rather than be doing homework. You can schedule homework time in the afternoon too. Preferably it is time that can be monitored in some way. Otherwise, teens may insist that they're spending time at the library or at their desk when they're actually hanging out with friends, which gives them opportunities to use drugs.

It is also important to think about structure in terms of how your family is organized. A family structure can be fairly rigid or flexible. It includes how clearly family roles are defined and how much reciprocity there is in those roles. Each family establishes the parameters that form the family organization from a range of possibilities. Each family subtly negotiates how separate or enmeshed family members are. Families also determine how isolated or interactive they are with one another and with the outside world. As is often the case, the extremes on either end of the spectrum may be less healthy while the middle range makes for optimal success.

Provide Strong Adult Roles

You know the expression, "Do as I say, not as I do." Well, that doesn't work with kids, especially with teens. They will watch you like a hawk. They will scrutinize and criticize your every move. Even if you were an absolutely perfect parent and human being, your teen would still find something wrong with you. Parenting is not an exact science. But if you want to steer your teen in the right direction, with a set of values and expectations for behavior, you had better be ready to follow that path yourself. Even though your teen is starting to move away from you and looking to peers for support, you are still his or her primary role model.

What you say is much less important than what you do. If you don't want your teen to swear, then don't swear, either. If you don't want him or her to lie, then you have to tell the truth. If you don't want your teen to abuse alcohol and other drugs, then don't let him or her see you drunk or stoned. You have to model the kinds of behaviors you want your teen to follow. You have to live the values you want your teen to internalize. To be a positive role model, you should practice integrity, courage, and curiosity in your daily life.

If your teen has been using substances and a mini-crisis has surfaced at home, you must find a way to be strong. This is a time when your teen needs your support and acceptance more than ever. He or she may be lost and looking for a way back to safety. You can provide that path by being there in every way possible. Think of your teen as someone caught in quicksand. That's what substance use is like. If you're frantically running around on the side, unsure of what to do, your child will keep sinking. But if you're a firmly rooted tree offering a branch that your child can grab onto, you may be able to help. Your child may flail around a bit and sink a little further, but if you stay steady, he or she will have somewhere to turn. If you remain a stable force, with patience and perseverance, you'll find a way to bring your child home safely.

Remember that you are the parent, and stick with that role. Many parents try to be friends with their teen. As your kids grow older, and especially once they move into adolescence, it may feel tempting to share confidences with them. Your teen is moving toward becoming an adult and sometimes even acting like one, so you may want to think of him or her as a peer. But your child doesn't need another friend. Hopefully he or she has plenty of friends already. What teens do need is a parent who can guide them into successful adulthood. They should be able to rely on you to help them figure out a way around the obstacles along the way. Your conversations can be meaningful, and you each can share your thoughts and feelings. Your role as a parent is to offer an experienced perspective and long-range view. For example, if your teen were to talk about getting a tattoo, a friend of his or hers might only consider how cool it would look. You, on the other hand, can talk about the long-term ramifications.

Think of the tactics you use to discipline your teen as part of your strategy in guiding him or her into adulthood. Try to see yourself as a gentle disciplinarian who uses consequences as teaching tools. These tools will help you in your role as an experienced guide who has already navigated and negotiated the uncharted territory your teen is entering.

Provide a Positive, Warm, Loving Environment

Optimal child development happens in homes that are full of love. Even young monkeys in research labs prefer a warm, soft "mother" to cuddle up to than an abundance of food. When these baby monkeys are given a choice between two wire "mothers" in their cages, they prefer the one covered in cloth to the one with food. They will actually give up food for warmth and love. Those infant monkeys with access to the cloth-covered figure grow at a more normal rate than monkeys who are only provided with the figure who provides food (Harlow and Zimmerman 1959). Babies in hospitals and orphanages who are deprived of physical affection will not grow normally, either. Once they are consistently shown affection through words and touch, they start growing at a normal rate again (Spitz 1946).

If teens are to grow to their full potential, they must feel that they are loved and valued. A study from the Center for Adolescent Health and Development at the University of Minnesota and the Carolina Population Center found that the more teens experience feeling loved by their parents, the less likely they are to smoke, abuse alcohol or drugs, engage in sex, be violent, or commit suicide (Resnick et al. 1997). Express your love openly, with physical contact and praise. It does wonders for teenagers' self-esteem to feel that their parents are proud of them and are willing to say so, both privately and in public.

Ideally, your love will be constant and unconditional. You may have heard the phrase, "Even when I'm mad at you, I still love you." Well, you've got to really mean it! An open expression of loving, caring feelings lets your teen know that even when you're unhappy with them or disappointed in their behavior, your deep regard for who they are remains intact. Find ways to support your teen's interests, and show that you're interested. Find out about that loud music you hear coming from his or her room. See if there are any lyrics, or a singer's voice, or a good guitar solo that you can find appealing (or at least tolerable) so that you'll be willing to listen with interest. Even if your child is interested in clothing or a philosophy you find strange, see if there are any aspects of those interests that you can learn about. The information may allow you to better understand your teen, and once you understand your child's point of view, you're in a better position to offer alternative views or opinions. Be sure to nurture those interests that you think are positive and healthy. If your teen wants to play the guitar, find ways to make it happen. Even if you're worried about the symbolism or underlying message of a certain kind of music or dance, if your teen wants to get involved in an interest like that, encourage it! Whatever the activity, it's preferable to having your teen doing drugs, isn't it?

When teens believe you love them, they will be more accepting of the decisions or restrictions you make for them about their use of drugs and alcohol. If teens believe that you feel an abundance of love for them, they will also believe that you have their best interests at heart when you respond to their using. When you restrict them or give them consequences for their behavior, they will know that you are doing it out of love. They won't think it's out of revenge, or taking pleasure in punishing them. If you decide to get them into a treatment program, they will be less likely to think you're just trying to get rid of them.

Provide Clear and Consistent Rules and Limits

A big part of providing structure for kids is making sure that everyone involved understands the rules and limits. You might assume that your kids know what you expect from them, but unless your rules are clearly stated, there will be a lot of room for misunderstanding. Since teens are frequently trying to push the limits, your rules must be crystal clear to them. There should be no ambiguity about your expectations, and for the most part, the rules should be firm. You can occasionally make exceptions to a particular rule, but the exception should be clearly stated, with the understanding that it would be a onetime change and not a new rule.

If there are two adults setting the rules, the two of you must agree on what those rules are. Outline what areas you want to consider, and discuss the parameters together, without your teen present. Think of all the basic areas you want covered. Curfew, chores, telephone and computer time, homework, friends, activities, and, of course, drug and alcohol use are some of the basic areas to consider. Make sure what is and what is not acceptable is clear between the two of you before ever presenting the rules to your child. State the rules in positive rather than negative terms. There should be more do's than don'ts (e.g., instead of saying, "Don't use the phone until your homework is done," state it by saying, "When your homework is done, you can have one hour of phone time").

Rules must be consistent. Although we realize there are occasional exceptions to most rules, in general, it's best to stick to what you have set up with your teen. And stick to it consistently over time. Too often, parents start to yield on the rules when their teen tries to test the limits. If your teen has been doing well for a few weeks, you can get drawn into thinking that now everything is fine and back to normal. Don't ease up on the rules. It may seem easier to let your teen come home after curfew or miss piano practice to go to a dance than to remind him or her of prior commitments, but if you remain consistent, you will teach your teen about perseverance, integrity, and responsibility.

Include Them in the Process

When dealing with younger children, you probably set all the rules with little or no input from your kids. When setting rules and limits for teens, however, it helps to include them in the process. This will help to teach them negotiation skills and how to compromise. It provides them with an opportunity to begin to have some control over their lives and to take responsibility for their behavior. Plus, when teens are involved in setting up the rules, they are more likely to abide by them. This does not mean that they set the rules themselves. Far from it. Generally, you should present your ideas about what rules are being covered and what your expectations are, and then ask for their thoughts and input. Doing so can make the process more workable.

Example: You have set an 11:00 P.M. weekend curfew for your son, but he has been coming home closer to 11:30 on Friday nights. Because he has been at a football game, you haven't been very firm about the time. Now he has started coming home closer to midnight.

You:	We've set an 11:00 curfew and you're consistently missing it. When we set a time for you to be home, we mean it. We don't think it's safe for you to be driving around late at night.
Your son:	There's not enough time after the game to get home by 11:00. By the time we leave the parking lot, swing by McDonald's drive-through, and I drop off Bruce and Sue, there's no way I can make it home by 11:00.
You:	What time could you be home?
Your son:	Oh, for sure by midnight.
You:	Midnight is too late. We're not comfortable with you driving home alone after dropping them off at that hour. You might just have to skip McDonald's.
Your son:	But . . .
You:	How about this. We'll make your curfew 11:30. We realize it's hard to get home by 11:00. But no exceptions. No coming in at 11:45, not even 11:32. That gives you an extra half hour to get home. Let's try that for a couple months and see how it goes. What do you think?
Your son:	Two whole months. That's crazy! How about one month?
You:	How about we stick with the 11:00 curfew and not change anything? You haven't been honoring your curfew. Until we see that you can, we're not considering anything else. If the two months go well, then we'll talk about giving you time to get something to eat after the game.
Your son:	Okay, okay. It's a deal.

Many parents find it works best to write out the rules. That way, there's less room for misunderstanding or manipulation, and less to argue about. With written rules, your teen will know exactly what's expected. Teens like to know what's expected and tend to do better when they do. The clearer your rules are, the better you will feel about them. If you feel good about the limits you've set, you're less likely to sway off course if a rule is broken.

Provide Rewards and Consequences

Not only do the rules and limits need to be clear, but you also must spell out what will happen if they're followed and what will happen if they're not. Don't wait until you see how your teen does with a rule before setting the rewards and consequences. For one thing, if both you and your teen know in advance what will happen if your teen breaks a rule, you will be more likely to follow through, rather than come down more harshly than you intended. You can also write down the rewards for good behavior and the consequences for not meeting expectations. This too will prevent manipulation by your teen and prevent you from faltering on your agreements.

It also helps if teens are included in coming up with the rewards and consequences. Especially the rewards. They know best what will motivate them. Get input from your teen. Your child can help you determine what things will deter him or her from behaving in a certain way. In any case, you have the final word on both rewards and consequences.

Whenever possible, rewards and consequences should fit the behavior you are addressing, and they should be delivered as quickly as possible after the fact. You may have standard responses that work with your teen, but sometimes those old standards don't make sense for the new rule your teen has broken. For instance, if your teen takes the car out and drives farther than you had agreed, taking away telephone privileges makes less sense than taking away car privileges.

Avoid Overprotection

Whatever you do, don't protect your teen from the natural consequences of his or her behavior. Too often, parents intervene on behalf of their child, only to eliminate the consequences that could help them change. An example we frequently hear involves the child getting up in the morning and getting to school on time. The scenario is this: Parent wakes teen in the morning to get ready for school. Teen tries to sleep in. Parent nags teen to wake up. Teen gets mad at the parent. Teen finally gets up, but now it is too late to catch the bus. So parent drives teen to school so he or she won't be tardy.

What about an alarm clock? What about having the teen take a later bus and arrive late to school? What about letting the teen get five or six tardies until the teacher lowers his or her grade? We know, in the short run, it seems better for your teen to get to class on time. But by coming to his or her aid, you're only allowing your child to continue being irresponsible.

You can still impose consequences at home for this behavior. And the consequences should be set up before your teen sleeps in the next time. If your son continues to get tardies, perhaps you won't allow him to go out on the weekend. Or maybe you will require your daughter to get off the telephone or computer earlier in the evening so she can get enough sleep.

Rewards should fit the behavior too. Using the previous example about setting a curfew, if your son came home by 11:30 on Friday nights for two months, you might reward him for being responsible. Here's what you might say

> Now that you've been coming home on time for two months, we'll re-negotiate your curfew. We can see that you've been much more responsible. We know you'd like to have time to get something to eat after the game. We're willing to try a midnight curfew for the next month to see how it goes. Since we are concerned about you driving alone after you drop off your friends, have your friends call us when you leave their house and head home, so we know exactly when to expect you.

As with consequences, it's important to stick to the rules for a period of time before giving any rewards for good behavior. Your son or daughter should have a positive track record for quite a while before you reward a change in behavior. After months of coming home late, two or three weeks of getting home on time are not enough proof of newfound responsibility. That doesn't mean that you shouldn't give praise immediately. Timely praise or even little rewards can help teens know they're on track and keep them going in a positive direction. Having rewards too far out in the future will make teens feel that they'll never be able to achieve their goals. Teens perceive time differently than adults. Two or three months can feel like an eternity. Telling teens that you'll review their behavior a year from now is too long a time and won't work.

Provide Acceptance

Adolescence is a new and different path. For the first time your son or daughter is relying more on his or her own judgment than on yours. Be realistic in your expectations. Teens are likely to hit some bumps along the way and will make wrong decisions at times. You may impose consequences for poor decisions, but do it with some understanding that learning how to make good decisions is a process. Your attitude is the key here. This is when your ability to separate your teen from his or her behavior is essential. Give your child encouragement to get it right next time. Have faith that as you discuss choices, your teen will think differently and try new choices in the future. Be sure to value a good effort. Emphasize that various struggles and failures are all opportunities to learn.

Similarly, you are also facing new territory in parenting a teen. You too will make mistakes along the way. It's okay to admit your mistakes to your child. In fact, it's great to admit your mistakes because it gives you an opportunity to apologize. You will teach your child about learning and growing by your example. Having the ability to grow through your children is a sign that you are a healthy, evolving human being. Try not to get down on yourself. Give yourself a break when you make a mistake. If you can do that for yourself, then you will be more likely to have that attitude with your teen. Self-acceptance leads to acceptance of others.

Work on Communication

Just as you must accept yourself in order to accept your teen, you must also be aware of your thoughts and feelings when talking and listening to your teen. Self-awareness is a useful tool in good communication. Pay attention to your thoughts and also to cues from your body. Check your breathing, your heart rate, and the tension in your body. If you're unaccustomed to being aware of your feelings, physical cues can give you helpful hints.

You also have to be willing to communicate in depth with your child. This means being willing to be honest and vulnerable. Letting yourself be vulnerable and encouraging your teen to open up to you takes a great deal of trust. Trust is built over a period of time, and since trust usually breaks down when a teen has used drugs and alcohol, it may take you some time to build it up again. Open, honest communication is an excellent way to rebuild that trust.

Use "I" messages whenever possible. Instead of simply pointing out your teen's behavior, include how that behavior affects you, and state what you'd like to see differently next time. Let's use the earlier example of your son coming in after curfew. Let's say he is an hour late, and you're filled with all kinds of horrible thoughts of car accidents, assaults, or whatever. Instead of yelling, "You're late, and you're grounded!" try saying, "When you're late like this, I get scared for your safety. I know I may be worried for nothing, but I'd really like you to get home on time or at least call and let me know where you are and that you're okay."

This "I " statement conveys what's going on inside you. You're not just angry and waiting to punish him. You're scared and worried and want him to be safe. That's why you've set a curfew. This kind of communication elicits your son's empathy and encourages an awareness of the impact of his behavior. You can still carry out the pre-set consequence for his missing the curfew, but you've shared the rationale for the rule and the consequence. You've turned the incident from one of right vs. wrong, or good vs. bad, to a lesson in responsibility and commitment to one another.

Practice Good Listening Skills

Most people think of a person with good communication skills as someone who has the ability to express him or herself and convey thoughts and feelings clearly. However, expressing yourself is only one side of the coin. A good communicator is also someone who can listen carefully. Make an effort to listen to everything that your teen is trying to say. Selective listening, choosing to hear only what you want to hear, prevents you from really "getting" what your teen has to say. It will be difficult to respond empathically or effectively if you don't have the whole picture. So listen first, and respond later. And if you're really listening, you will also be teaching your teen to listen to you.

Reflective or active listening is a technique taught in many parenting classes. Initially, the technique can seem quite awkward. With practice however, it can be very effective. Reflective listening is used to elicit further information from the speaker and to see if you've understood what was being communicated. It's essential to avoid being judgmental. You also have to refrain from interjecting your point of view. Your goal is to try to experience what your teen is saying as if you were in his or her shoes. Use expressions like, "Sounds like you think . . . ?" "Are you saying that . . . ?" "Do you mean that . . . ?" Even though your teen might initially think it's very weird that you're talking this way, it will give him or her the sense that you're really trying to understand. It's a great feeling to not only be heard but to be understood.

After you have truly listened to your son or daughter, it will be your turn to respond. Understanding your teen's thoughts and emotions doesn't mean you have to think or feel the same way, however. You can acknowledge that the other person thinks your rules are too strict, but you don't have to agree. After hearing your teen's frustration, anger, embarrassment, etc., it is still your right to enforce the limits and explain why you have the rules that you do. This isn't about who's right and who's wrong.

Establishing a good communication channel with your teen creates an avenue for the two of you to resolve any conflicts you are having. Similarly, if you are skillfully communicating with your partner or other adults involved in your teen's life, conflicts will be dealt with more easily. Conflict resolution involves speaking skills, listening skills, thinking skills, and self-awareness. Developing these skills will allow you to solve problems in a peaceful manner while maintaining respect for yourself and your teen.

To make this work, the two of you will have to agree on a few basic ground rules. The first rule is to agree that you are both working to solve the problem. The second is to wait until both of you are calm and thinking clearly. Wait until you have cooled off from any angry exchanges before trying to solve anything. The third rule is to treat each other with respect. Don't interrupt one another.

Keep in mind that each person has a different perception of the same event. When witnesses of a crime are asked to describe what they saw, frequently there will be as many descriptions of the event as there are people being interviewed.

Again, what is most important is to listen and talk to each other honestly about your thoughts and feelings. Try to find out what you both need to bring about a feeling of resolution. Brainstorm solutions, even if some of them seem silly or outrageous. Sometimes the best thinking can be done when you free up your ideas. Then choose the solutions you like the best and make a plan you can both live with.

Develop Unity and Shared Goals

Teens need a sense of belonging to feel secure. They need to feel that they are part of something greater than they are. Teens who don't feel a sense of belonging at home often reach out to friends or even gangs in order to get that connection. As a parent, keep in mind that teens are doing a balancing act between the need for a sense of belonging at home and a need to strike out on their own.

Just because your teen is questioning or even rejecting some of what you are providing at home doesn't mean he or she will throw it all away in the end. You want to instill a commitment to the family that will last throughout his or her lifetime. Your shared history creates a deep bond that you can nurture and develop. Family experiences, large and small, good and bad, are a part of that history. These experiences, woven into the fabric of your family's life, give a unique identity that is your family's alone. Reflect on these experiences with your teen to show the importance of what it means to be in your family. Vacations, time with relatives, even sorrowful times, like funerals, add to the feelings of connection and unity.

Maintaining a value system shared by the family is critical. Identify those values that are important in your family. It doesn't matter whether those include giving to charities, getting a good education, or exercising regularly. What does matter is that you all acknowledge and live by those values. Abiding by the ethical principles that your family believes in is also essential: honesty, family loyalty, caring for elders, and so on. Each family has a different set of values and ethics. Stating them clearly and living by them in your daily lives creates a unifying force. For some families, a spiritual or religious orientation gives a sense of unity.

Family discussions focused on values that are applied to everyday situations will foster a sense of belonging and family commitment. Some families have designed a family crest or a family creed to identify what they stand for as a family. This is an exercise that can be fun and at the same time serve as an affirmation of what it is like to be in your family.

Show a High Regard for Honesty

Change includes risk taking and cannot take place without trust. Trust is encouraged when people feel free to honestly express their feelings. Trust is built when people do what they say they're going to do. Trust is built when people follow through on their commitments.

Know thyself. This is the first step in being able to speak openly and honestly. If you can speak from the heart and let the other person really know you, it is more likely that they will be open as well. The more comfortable you are with being yourself and with feeling okay about the person you are, the more honest and revealing of yourself you will be.

Letting your teen know your inner thoughts and feelings is a scary prospect for many parents. When your kids were smaller, you protected them from what was really going on inside of you. And rightly so. However, as children begin to grow up and mature, they are able to handle more information than when they were small. Can you find ways to be intimate with your teen? Can you share experiences that have been hard for you? Choices you had to make, people you had to leave behind, your hurts and your triumphs? Can you share your deep love and concern for your teen? Even when he or she is acting in ways that you can't stand? Can you share your fears for your teen? Your willingness to share yourself can serve as a great model for his or her development. Intimacy is a crucial part of relationships. It allows connection and safety. Taking the risk of allowing someone to really know you, warts and all, and coming out feeling accepted and loved, enables you to move through the world with more confidence.

This is not to suggest that you share everything with your teen. Please remember the importance of boundaries which we've outlined. Your teen is not your confidant or companion. There are many things about your own life, both present and past, that are best not shared. It is also important to keep in mind that what you share with a seventeen-year-old may be very different than what you share with a thirteen- or fourteen-year-old. Use discretion in what you share.

Parents frequently ask about sharing information regarding their own use of alcohol and drugs when they were teenagers. Again, discretion is advised. Whether or not to disclose past drug and alcohol use to your teen requires some serious thought. You make decisions every day about whether to share or not, in all kinds of situations. If you want to share something intimate about yourself, you usually consider how the revelation will feel to you and what impact it will have on the other person and your relationship with them. We all decide on a regular basis if we want to be open and vulnerable or closed and safe. Sharing something about yourself, like your use of drugs and alcohol, can leave you feeling more vulnerable.

Disclosing information is never neutral, and when you share information about yourself with your teen, it will always have an impact on them. Sharing your past use of drugs and alcohol with your teen could make your teen feel closer to you. It might make your teen feel like he or she is being treated like an adult. It could also give your teen an excuse to act out and justify using drugs. Through the context of your relationship with your teen, you will need to assess and predict how the information might be processed and used. Part of that assessment will depend on the age of your teen. Younger teens may not be far enough along in their moral and intellectual development to process the subtleties you are presenting. Disclosure of your use of substances may be taken as a license to use drugs. "If you did it, why can't I?" is a typical response younger teens give when they hear that kind of information. As for teens who have been using drugs for a while, you should remember that their development may be arrested. Although they are chronologically seventeen years of age, their moral and intellectual development may mean they still process information as if they were thirteen. You know your teen best. You have to assess how he or she will use the information.

Provide Healthy Rituals

Family rituals are very valuable for creating unity and cohesiveness. Rituals are a part of the structure you can provide to make your teen feel safe. Marking events, like birthdays, anniversaries, or holidays, with rituals that are repeated year after year helps children feel that they are a part of something larger. Sadly, as children get older, families frequently do away with everyday or weekly rituals. Celebration of holidays, outings to visit relatives, even family dinners fall by the wayside, as family members get busier and teens become more independent.

Shared activities help to establish your family identity. It's a way to bond around common interests. The activities don't always have to include every family member. It's okay for dad to regularly go to a baseball game with the kids, or to take his daughter ice-skating every Saturday. But everyone in the family should share some activities. Whether it's watching a movie together, playing cards, a board game, or even shopping at the mall, find some activities that everyone can enjoy. Establishing a weekly family meeting is a great way to connect with one another. It doesn't have to be a heavy time for people to air their differences (although many families use family meetings in this way). It can simply be a time to share the events of the week and to remind one another of upcoming schedules. If nothing else, maintain family dinners as a commitment to the family that everyone must keep. Sitting around the table together is a way to allow casual conversation in a nurturing environment that everyone can count on. If scheduling nightly dinners together is too hard, set up family dinners at least twice each week.

Designate Responsibilities

Teens are always asking to be treated more like adults, especially as they move into later adolescence. They also ask for more freedom. The amount of freedom given to teens and your view of them as mature, emerging adults should depend on how responsibly they handle themselves. Adulthood entails taking on more responsibility. Until you can be sure that your son or daughter is responsible about his or her commitments and can be counted on, treating your teen as an adult would be premature.

Greater responsibility can lead to more privileges, which then leads to more freedom. But until you feel comfortable with your teen's level of maturity (ability to be responsible) you should be cautious about the privileges and amount of freedom you allow.

Start Small

In order to assess your teen's level of maturity and how much responsibility he or she is ready to assume, begin with small tasks. As teens prove that they can meet the challenges of increasing responsibility, you can begin to give more privileges, more freedom, and treat them as more mature individuals. To test their level of responsibility, give them realistic tasks and chores to complete. A sign of responsibility is their ability to complete these tasks on their own. When you ask your son to carry in a package for you from the car, you should not have to ask several times before it gets done. Many teens may need a reminder here and there, but if you find yourself nagging them to do their chores, they are not showing responsibility. If you've asked your daughter to telephone you if there is a change of plans when she's out with her friends, and she forgets to do so, she is not acting responsibly. In fact, you will *really* know your teen is being responsible when he gets up from watching the TV on his own accord to carry in that package. Or when you get a phone call, without having to ask, from your daughter telling you her plans. Or better yet, imagine your teen phoning to ask if he or she can stop and pick up anything for you on the way home. Yes! There are teens who begin to assume this kind of responsibility.

Once your teen exhibits more responsibility, it will make sense to give him or her more freedom. As you begin to establish a hierarchy of responsibilities, you can set up a hierarchy of privileges and freedoms as well. With each new responsibility taken on and fulfilled, you can add another privilege.

Only when teens start acting like adults should they be treated like adults. Too often, teens think that being an adult just means having all the freedoms adults have. They haven't learned that being an adult means assuming responsibilities and commitments. Here is your opportunity to teach them.

Stay Informed

An important tool in dealing with drug abuse is acquiring knowledge about a variety of recovery concepts. Getting information about the effects of drugs on your brain, the hereditary aspects of addiction, and the stages of teen use of substances will help combat drug abuse. This book serves as a useful primer. We've also provided an annotated resource list in appendix B. Parenting classes and drug information classes are also offered through schools, churches, and community centers, such as the YMCA. Many treatment programs offer an education component for teens and families that are separate from enrollment in their full programs.

Both you and your teen need to learn as much as you can about the situation you find yourselves in. Learning both individually and as a family can be very rewarding. It's another way for your family to grow together and become closer. As you acquire more information, it gives you opportunities to open up the dialogue between you. When you are open to learning something new, you are showing your teen that you don't know everything. This admission is a good thing; it shows that you believe change is possible.

Have Fun and Use Humor

The family that laughs together stays together. Your family is facing a tough time. Even when teens are in the earliest stages of use, families spend a lot of time and energy getting through the problem. When families are confronted by any kind of crisis, it's easy to get caught up in the seriousness and gravity of the situation. And it is serious business, no question about it. However, allowing yourself to get bogged down with the crisis too fully will make it hard to lift yourselves out of the mess. A little lightness can be useful to get through the problem. It's helpful to balance the seriousness of the situation with laughter.

Make fun activities and ways to laugh together a part of your plan to bring your teen and your family back to health. They can be large and monumental activities or small but still meaningful ones. After an argument that took over an hour to get through, go have an ice cream together. If you're working with a family therapist for a period of time or have completed an education class together as a family, celebrate your accomplishments by treating the family to an outing of some kind.

Humor can be used as a way to deal with stressful situations. Perhaps the best way to use humor in a tense situation is to find ways to laugh at yourself. If you can laugh at yourself, it shows that you are self-aware and able to forgive yourself. When you can forgive yourself, you'll be able to forgive others too. When you don't take yourself too seriously, you'll find it easier to move on from a difficult situation.

It's important not to use humor at your teen's expense, especially when your teen's self-confidence is fragile. Humor in this case only leads to mistrust and increased tension, which will close down communication channels. It can make your teen feel worse about themselves and distrustful of you. But if you can find the absurdity in a situation and make light of it in a way that is not disrespectful, your teen will appreciate it too.

We've heard wonderful stories from families about finding ways to use humor. A mother and her son, in the throes of a heated argument, were startled by a loud noise of two cats fighting outside. This allowed them to take a step back and see their own behavior and how funny they sounded. They looked at each other and broke out in laughter. It eased the tension and brought them closer together. The humor allowed them to put the argument in perspective. They were reminded of how much they really cared for one another and how unimportant the content of the argument was in comparison to their bond. Another family shared a story of two siblings loudly arguing and trying to one-up each other. When they were younger, the two would tease each other by sticking their tongues out at each other. In the middle of this very intense argument, they started to tease each other in the same way. And mom and dad joined in too! They began a contest to see who could stick out their tongue the farthest, rather than arguing. They all ended up laughing and rolling on the floor. What argument? Right?

A Note About Self-Care

Parents regularly ask us how to deal with a drug using teen. What's the best approach, when do I intervene, and what form of treatment is best? All are good questions to ask. The focus is solely on their child and what to do to help them. These parents are committed and diligent in their efforts. And they are drained, spent, and exhausted. They are so busy taking care of their teen that they forget to take care of themselves.

You've got to find ways to keep yourself afloat through this ordeal. You will be little help to your teen if you aren't sleeping nights, are getting distracted at work, or find yourself arguing with loved ones on what you should do. Be sure to take time to refuel. You'll need to remain strong and focused to get yourself through this.

Many of the suggestions described in this book can be helpful to you. Getting support from those around you, be they friends, family, or other parents going through the same struggles, is essential. Don't go it alone. Support groups that can help you learn how to let go and stay calm and clear-headed are useful.

Take time for yourself. Try not to be a slave to your teen by having to watch over him or her every minute. You still deserve a night out with friends or an hour at the gym now and again. Find those things that sustain you and continue to integrate them into your routine.

If you are so worried about your teen that you're afraid to leave him or her at home alone, find someone who can come and stay for a few hours. Many parents will have a child go stay with others for a weekend, or even longer, to get the respite they need. Your family and friends may be more than happy to help out. And your teen may be just as thrilled to get a break from you. Other adults who you both care about and trust can help you both through this difficult time.

Know your limits and honor them. It's okay to say no to someone pulling on you for favors, whether it's your teen or someone else. You'll have to decide what you can handle and what feels like too much right now. Only when you take care of yourself will you be in a position to truly be there for your child.

Putting It All Together

For a teen in the early stages of substance use, you are the best treatment program money can buy. Your teen can change his or her behavior and begin to thrive again right in the comfort of your own home. If you catch the problem early enough and implement changes to your home environment, there will be no need for your teen to go further along the continuum of drug use. Don't wait for the problem to grow to insurmountable proportions.

When your teen is in the early stages of using substances, there may be no reason for a referral to a drug treatment program. But there is reason to address the drug-using behavior immediately and firmly. If your child had a cold, you wouldn't go to the hospital, but you also wouldn't ignore the symptoms or let your child go out in the rain without a jacket. And you certainly wouldn't wait until the cold turned into pneumonia before doing something about it. You can make a difference starting right now.

CHAPTER 8

What to Do If Your Teen Is Abusing Alcohol or Drugs

In this chapter we suggest ways to deal with your teen if his or her substance use has reached a level that would be classified as abuse (see items 13–38 on the Parent's Awareness Checklist in chapter 1). This is a teen whose involvement with drugs and alcohol has progressed beyond the stage of experimentation or regular use. Things are getting serious now. Your teen's behavior requires a strong parental response and often the help of professionals. You must now refine those skills, such as clear communication and setting limits, that were useful in the earlier stages of your teen's drug use. And you will have to crank it up a notch.

Practice Tough Love

Professionals often counsel parents to respond with tough love. First of all, it's necessary to distinguish between *tough love* and the TOUGHLOVE organization. Tough love is a style of responding to children. It refers to a continuum of behaviors that can range from the first time you say no to a child's request for more ice cream to the much tougher decision of sending your drug-abusing teen to a boot camp–style residential treatment facility. TOUGHLOVE refers to a national self-help movement started by Phyllis and David York and Ted Wachtel. We'll discuss both.

The tough love approach is not for everyone. It is certainly not for parents who are passive and feel unable to set tough limits for their child, even with group support. It's most useful for parents who are struggling to regain control of their home environment, and are willing to take a stand.

If you're tired of bending over backwards and giving your teen another "last" chance, you're ready for tough love. If you've already begun to set limits and assign consequences for misbehavior as described in the last chapter, you're already on the tough love track. Taking a tough love approach can help remedy a situation where there is a serious problem involving drugs or alcohol, and the teen appears to be in charge. Practicing tough love is a way of taking care of yourself. It's a way of protecting yourself from being abused and victimized by your out-of-control teen. And it may save your child's life.

Use Assertive Communication

To practice tough love, you need to be able to communicate assertively. To put this in context, assertive communication is one of three parental communication styles: the other two styles are passive communication and aggressive communication.

Parents using a passive communication style will typically say nothing about their teen's behavior. Their fervent wish is that things will improve on their own, or that the teen will simply "grow out of it." They are unwilling to confront the teen. They don't want to rock the proverbial boat, fearing that by doing so they will only make things worse. This is not an effective strategy. It allows the teen to progress along the continuum of drug abuse. The teen is deprived of parental guidance.

Parents using an aggressive communication style will tend to yell and shout. They will rage at teens, loudly telling them how bad they are and how wrong their behavior is. They freely assign blame and try to make the teen feel guilty. This communication style is bound to backfire. The teen will either respond aggressively, thereby escalating the exchange, or worse, retreat into sullen silence.

Parents using an assertive communication style have the best chance of making an impact on their drug-abusing teen. Assertive communication allows you to express your thoughts and feelings. It also allows you to stand up for your parental rights and set healthy limits.

An assertive statement consists of three parts: I think, I feel, and I want. The "I think" component consists of a description of what you see or notice. It states the facts while avoiding blame or judgment. The "I feel" component describes your honest emotional reaction without trying to make the other person feel defensive. Finally, the "I want" component of an assertive statement includes making a specific request for a new kind of behavior. Here's an example:

> Kevin, this is the third time this month that you've come home after curfew, smelling of alcohol and slurring your speech. I'm scared to death. I'm really worried about your drinking, and where it might lead. I want you to come with me to see a drug abuse counselor and get an evaluation.

Rules, Family Contracts, and Consequences

As long as your children are living in your house, you are responsible for providing them with food, shelter, and a safe environment. It's only reasonable to expect something from them in return; i.e., that they follow the rules. Most families have a loose set of rules that are usually vague and have loopholes as big as the Grand Canyon. That works out all right for most intact and functional families. However, when things start to go wrong, when a teen begins to abuse drugs and act out, it's time to do something different. It's time to have a family meeting and discuss a basic set of rules that everyone will follow.

If this does not produce the desired result, the next step is for the family to sit down and hammer out a written contract, one with consequences. The purpose of a written contract is to avoid ambiguity and to clearly state expectations. While a typical family contract may include a range of subjects, including chores (taking out the garbage, doing the dishes, etc.), we'll just focus here on problematic teen behaviors.

First, the family contract needs a preamble that spells out a commitment to honesty and absolutely no physical or verbal abuse among family members. This is nonnegotiable and serves as a safety net for further interactions. Typically three items addressed in the family contract are curfews, cutting classes, and use of illicit substances.

Curfews should be determined by the age of the teen and are open for negotiation. You may also want to negotiate the possibility of rare extended curfews for special events. Once you've come to an agreement, you need to assign consequences for noncompliance. Consequences may include loss of car privileges or being grounded for a period of time. Be careful, though. Make sure that you are willing to follow through on the consequences. Loss of a teen's car privileges may require you to become an unwilling chauffeur. Grounding a teen over the weekend may turn you into a reluctant prison guard.

Cutting classes is a real warning sign and should be taken seriously. Since your teen is not where he or she is supposed to be, your teen could be anywhere, doing anything. It's helpful to establish a relationship with the school guidance counselor or principal. Ask whoever is in charge to contact you if unauthorized absences occur. As a consequence for this behavior, you might insist that your teen come directly home from school for several weeks. Of course, this scenario would require that there is a parent or another responsible adult at home and available in the afternoon to monitor compliance. Another option is to require your teen to attend a structured supervised activity, like a tutoring program.

Establish a rule of zero tolerance for any drug use other than drugs prescribed by a physician. This includes smoking and drinking any alcoholic beverages for teens under the legal age. If you're not sure whether or not your teen is using, consider using a home drug-testing kit. If your teen fails to comply with the zero tolerance drug-use rule, you should take him or her to a professional for a drug-abuse evaluation. It's important that you communicate to your teen that this will be the consequence of his or her failure to comply with your rule.

Use TOUGHLOVE

TOUGHLOVE (International) is a non-profit corporation dedicated to providing ongoing education and support for parents and teens. The organization began with a book written in 1982, based on the personal experiences of Phyllis and David York, in Doylestown, Pennsylvania. Both licensed family therapists, they were faced with two out-of-control daughters who were getting drunk, running away, and finally getting arrested. Their story was dramatized in the 1985 movie, *Toughlove*, which drew some bad publicity and caused a lot of misunderstanding.

On the TOUGHLOVE Web site (listed in appendix B), the organization is quick to explain that it does not offer a quick fix and definitely does not advocate or support:

- throwing kids out

- violence against kids or parents

- verbal abuse by kids or parents

One of the organization's more important contributions is the idea of a Parent's Bill of Rights. For example, you as a parent have the right to a good night's sleep, a sleep undisturbed by worrying about where your child is or the fear of being awakened by a drunken or stoned teen in the middle of the night. You have the right to not be treated badly and to expect courtesy and cooperation from all family members living in your home. You are not required to accept violent or inconsiderate behavior from your teen. And you are certainly not required to continue to bail your teen out financially by paying his or her fines.

The organization also subscribes to a set of core beliefs. Foremost among them is that parents are people too. And that parents and kids are not equal. TOUGHLOVE acknowledges that parenting is a two-way street. A teen's behavior has an effect on parents, and parent's behavior has an effect on their kids. The organization recognizes that blaming, either your self or others, is never helpful. Most importantly however, it emphasizes that family problems are rooted in the culture, and that the solution is for families to give and get support in their own community.

That's right. You're not alone. You're not the first family to be afflicted with an out-of-control drug-abusing teen. TOUGHLOVE has organized an extensive support network with parent groups available throughout the country. And recently it has expanded its presence internationally as well. These groups are made up of parents just like you—parents who have been there and can sympathize with your dilemma.

TOUGHLOVE support groups get started in several ways. Sometimes a group is started by a couple of families who have read the book, *Toughlove*. Sometimes it's a mental health professional who specializes in work with adolescents and families who gets the ball rolling. The organization sponsors weekend workshops in various locations in the United States and Canada. The goal of these workshops is to train parents and professionals to practice TOUGHLOVE effectively.

TOUGHLOVE suggests that the basic elements of successful groups include the following:

- Meetings are held in a community space, not a group member's home. A public meeting space is more accessible and businesslike. It also avoids problems with privacy.

- Parents should be responsible for the group. If a mental health professional has set up the group, he or she should back off as soon as the group is established and viable on its own.

- Meetings should be structured to allow time for a) check-in, b) success stories, c) sharing information or guest speakers, d) helping individual families develop a specific plan, and e) support for parents taking action.

- If the group gets too large, it can split up into subgroups for part of the meeting.

Note: For parents who are looking for support but who are not ready to buy the whole TOUGHLOVE package, there are a number of other options. First, there's Al-Anon, a twelve-step program for family members of addicted loved ones. You may also want to contact your church, synagogue, or other religious institution, your local school district, or your parks and recreation department to find out about parent support groups. HMOs can also be a good source of information.

Can You Trust Your Teen?

It's always sad when trust erodes in a family. And it's good to give your teen the benefit of the doubt, up to a point. It's a sad thing when parents feel they have to invade their teen's privacy to get at the truth. But it's also good to know when a change in tactics is in order.

When to Snoop

All teens lie to their parents sometimes. Lying only becomes really problematic when it's part of a pattern of deception designed to hide dangerous behavior. This is particularly true when that dangerous behavior involves the abuse of drugs or alcohol.

Before you become a snoop, sit your teen down to explain your concerns and give him or her a fair warning. Using the principles of assertive communication already discussed, you should say something along these lines:

> *Crystal, I've noticed that your grades have gone down and all your new friends seem to be getting in trouble all the time. I'm worried about you, and I'm afraid that you're doing drugs. So I want to warn you that I'm going to start snooping around. If you drop your coat on the floor, I'm going to go through your pockets before I hang it up. If you leave your backpack lying around, I'm going to go through that too. And if I have to clean up your room, I'm going to keep my eyes open for suspicious stuff.*

Partnership for a Drug-Free America produced a very effective public service spot on television, featuring a series of teens seemingly attacking their parents.

"You invaded my privacy," says one teen.

"My *privacy*," says another teen.

"I hated it," says another.

"I hated you," says another.

"I thought you were the worst parents," says another.

The spot ends unexpectedly with a teen looking straight into the camera and saying with obvious sincerity, "Thanks."

Home Drug Testing

Parents should consider carefully before ordering and using a home drug-testing kit. The clear implication is that you've lost trust in your teen and that you aren't able to detect, on your own, whether or not he or she is lying to you. Of course, that may be precisely the reason why you're ordering the testing kit. One way to frame the situation with teens is to tell them that the test can restore trust by providing them with an opportunity to prove their innocence.

Home drug-testing kits, which require a urine sample, can let parents know immediately (within five minutes) if their child is using illicit drugs. The kit will provide information on the presence of a range of substances, including opiates, cocaine, marijuana, and even stimulants and depressants. These testing kits are available at local pharmacies or on the Internet, for a reasonable price, usually around ten dollars per test. In some areas of the country, Bedford County, Tennessee, for example, local government officials are providing home testing kits free of charge, one per family.

A teen who is trying to conceal his or her drug use may also try to beat the test by using any of a number of adulterants. Fortunately, a company called Home Health Testing sells dipping strips called TamperTest which are designed to detect urine adulteration. This product even tests for specific gravity levels. Some teens drink a lot of water, or even add water to the container, in an attempt to dilute the sample so drug levels will fall below detectable thresholds. TamperTest also checks for pH and creatinine levels, as well as for the presence of nitrites and oxidants which might interfere with an accurate reading.

Please keep in mind that home drug-testing kits are not 100 percent reliable. Parents must read and follow the directions carefully and exercise caution to avoid contamination, which might lead to inaccurate test results. If the teen insists that the test is giving a false positive you can confirm the results with a second home test. If you really want to be on the safe side, you can send a urine sample to a certified laboratory for confirmation. Lab tests will be more expensive (between $50 and $75), but they are very reliable and rarely have false positive results.

Getting Professional Help

At a certain point, you may decide to seek professional help. Perhaps you've reached this decision because your teen broke some family rules. Perhaps you've reached it after testing your teen for drug use. Or maybe you've discovered drugs or paraphernalia in the house. You know that something unhealthy is going on. You're just not sure what it is or what to do about it. The fist step is to have your teen professionally evaluated for drug abuse.

Drug Abuse Evaluation

You first need to find a competent agency or professional to do the evaluation. This is an important decision, so don't just go to the Yellow Pages and pick someone at random. And don't call the telephone number from that advertisement you saw on the television screen. You should do a little bit of research first. If you belong to an HMO, ask if there is a chemical dependency unit, hopefully with an adolescent component. Or talk to your teen's school counselor about getting a referral. Counselors usually have the benefit of experience and may have a list of professionals who have helped other parents in a similar situation.

Another reliable resource is the National Directory of Drug Abuse and Alcohol Treatment and Prevention Programs. This catalogue is usually available in your local library. If it's not, you can call the Department of Health and Human Services in Washington, D.C. (see appendix B) to request a copy for yourself.

SAMHSA is another reliable source of information (the Web site is listed in appendix B). Follow the links to the Substance Abuse Treatment Facility Locator and request information about adolescent treatment programs. Type in your zip code and you will get a list of the ten nearest programs in your area, anywhere in the USA.

Once you've chosen an agency or professional, call and have a conversation before making an appointment. Communicate your concerns about your teen and be prepared to list the behaviors you find troubling. Ask specifically if the evaluations offered differentiate between teens who have psychological problems and those who are abusing drugs and alcohol. You want to work with someone who specializes in assessing teen behaviors and also has experience in the field of chemical dependency.

The assessment itself should gather information from the teen, the parents, and the school. A comprehensive assessment includes an evaluation of the physical, psychological, social, intellectual, and emotional development of the teen. This usually involves a physical examination and a battery of psychological tests. Sometimes a drug test is required as well. A thorough drug-abuse evaluation will take some time.

The final step in the process is always the summary conference. This is where it all comes together, and the professional reports his or her findings. Basically, this means giving you an assessment of where your teen falls on the drug use/drug abuse/dependency continuum. The report should also include a diagnosis, along with an identifying code, taken from the latest edition of the *Diagnostic and Statistical Manual of Mental Disorders* (popularly known as the *DSM-IV*) (APA 1994).

Don't be scared by the term *diagnosis*. A diagnosis helps you name your teen's problem, and the nice thing about the *DSM-IV* is that it stipulates the necessary behavioral criteria which must be present to make a particular diagnosis. This makes for consistency and protects teens from being arbitrarily labeled and railroaded into unnecessary treatment.

Treatment Options

If the drug-abuse evaluation results in the conclusion that your teen is in need of outside help, you will be presented with a range of therapeutic recommendations. These treatment options should be dictated by the severity of the diagnosis.

Self-Help

In addition to a treatment recommendation, the first suggestion is usually to try a self-help group. That means sending your son or daughter to a twelve-step meeting. Alcoholics Anonymous (AA), Narcotics Anonymous (NA), and even Marijuana Anonymous (MA) meetings are readily available. And the price is right (free of charge, donation requested but not required). The first three steps of these twelve-step programs can help substance-abusing teens to become more honest, decide to stop using drugs, and start a new course of action. Steps four through nine encourage the teen to be honestly introspective, change their behavior, and rectify past mistakes where possible and desirable. Steps ten through twelve are designed to help the teen continue a program of recovery. AA and NA recommend that beginners do "ninety in ninety"—attend ninety meetings in the first ninety days—and get a sponsor to help them work the steps.

Parents are usually encouraged to attend Al-Anon meetings. These meetings are designed to help and support family members who are affected by the alcohol or drug abuse of a loved one. Meetings often focus on codependency issues. Not as available as Al-Anon, but just as useful, is Families Anonymous. Founded in 1971, there are over 500 registered groups worldwide, over 200 of which meet in this country.

Historically, Alcoholics Anonymous was founded by Bill W. and Dr. Bob, two alcoholics who started talking together instead of drinking. Interestingly, Carl Jung had an early influence on AA. One of Jung's patients, in 1931, kept relapsing into alcoholism. After a year of this, Jung declared that medical and psychiatric treatment was unlikely to prove helpful and that the only hope was in a genuine spiritual awakening. In a letter written to Bill W. in 1961, Jung states the famous dictum, "spiritus contra spiritum," which translates from the Latin into, "spirituality against [alcoholic] spirits."

Narcotics Anonymous, Cocaine Anonymous, and Marijuana Anonymous were spin-offs of AA and follow a similar twelve-step approach. When people with drug-abuse problems first started attending AA meetings, there was an attitude that these other substance abusers didn't belong in a place where people were trying to get sober from alcohol. The new organizations filled the need for those folks who might not have a problem with drinking but still needed the help a twelve-step program provides. Now, with so many people using both alcohol and other drugs, the division is no longer necessary, and people with drug problems readily attend AA meetings.

For people turned off by the references to a "higher power" in AA, there are also programs available which make do without spirituality. Rational Recovery (RR) and Secular Organizations for Sobriety (SOS) offer support to alcohol- and drug-abusing atheists and agnostics.

All of these organizations should be listed in your local telephone directory. When you call, you will either get a helpful live person or a recorded message giving you dates, times, and locations of meetings in your area. When you go to the first meeting, there will be lists of other meetings available to you.

Outpatient Treatment

When a teen is diagnosed with a substance-abuse problem—for example, cannabis abuse (*DSM-IV* code 305.20)—the recommendation is usually outpatient drug treatment. This consists primarily of group therapy sessions with a licensed professional. Individual therapy sessions with a licensed counselor often supplement the group therapy and delve into deeper issues. Groups of teens with similar substance-abuse problems meet together to discuss alternatives to drug use and support each other in being drug free. The therapy group provides a safe place where teens can interact and learn to disclose things about themselves, build trust, and form meaningful relationships. Unfortunately, in these contexts, teens can sometimes learn to "talk the talk," to say the thing that the counselor wants to hear.

These therapy groups can serve as a complement to attendance at twelve-step meetings. Also be aware that any good outpatient treatment program has a family education component. In addition, family therapy sessions are usually required. It's also helpful for parents to have regular meetings with the teen's counselor or therapist at the outpatient facility.

Inpatient Drug Treatment

When a teen is diagnosed as being drug dependent—for example, alcohol dependent (*DSM-IV* code number 303.90)—the standard recommendation is for inpatient drug treatment, often in a hospital setting. The teen lives in the facility under twenty-four-hour supervision. When the drug dependency includes physical addiction, the inpatient program can provide drug detoxification (medically supervised withdrawal) in a safe, controlled environment. Inpatient programs usually require participation in daily therapy groups. Stays are typically limited to a twenty-eight-day period and are often covered by medical insurance. Having the appropriate *DSM-IV* diagnosis can be helpful in getting reimbursement from your insurance company.

The inpatient program that you choose for your teen should be certified by the Joint Commission on the Accreditation of Health Care Organizations (JCAHO). This organization has strict guidelines for high quality health care that includes substance abuse-treatment. To assure that teens are treated with respect, JCAHO makes periodic on-site visits to treatment providers. It also checks to make sure that the provider develops and implements adequate treatment plans.

Residential Treatment

Residential treatment programs are usually recommended as a follow-up to the inpatient program. Length of stay can range from a minimum of three months to a maximum of one to two years. Sometimes when drug detoxification is not needed, the teen may be referred directly to a residential program. Most adolescent residential treatment programs are structured along the lines of a therapeutic community and modeled after Synanon. In fact, Daytop Village in New York, a program which has helped over 100,000 individuals, was cofounded in 1963 by David Deitch, a Synanon graduate.

An adolescent therapeutic community is a highly structured drug-free environment where teens recovering from alcohol and drug-abuse problems all work together. The therapeutic community, which includes both professional and paraprofessional staff, comprises the village it takes to raise a drug-free individual. An important part of the community is the inclusion of program graduates who have completed additional training in counseling and serve as role models for recovering teens.

Treatment in a therapeutic community usually consists of three stages. In the first stage the teen learns the values, norms, and language of the community. Typically, no communication with the outside world is allowed for the first several weeks. A new member starts at the bottom, literally. The first assignment is often mopping floors. Gradually, as the teen demonstrates responsibility, job assignments improve. The middle stage of treatment in a therapeutic community involves self-exploration and the adoption of new attitudes and behaviors. Throughout their treatment, teens are regularly seen by a therapist who may do individual and family therapy when appropriate. There is also a strong educational and vocational program in place to help prepare teens for the future. The final stage is reentry to the broader community. Teens in this stage begin to reintegrate into the outside world by working and having increased visits with family while they are still living in the community and getting support from their peers and staff. An aftercare program usually involves living off campus in a halfway house with other program graduates or returning to live at home while still attending evening or weekend groups at the program.

More intensive and restrictive therapeutic options will be discussed in the next chapter.

CHAPTER 9

What to Do If Your Teen Won't Cooperate

You've tried everything humanly possible. Your teen won't listen to you. He or she comes home at all hours and sometimes doesn't even come home at all. He or she often pukes in the bathroom, stinks from alcohol, or reeks of marijuana. He or she has refused to go into a treatment program or has stopped attending one that your family started. Your teen just laughs at your attempts to set consequences for misbehavior, and shouts curses at you when you try to take a stand. Is this it? Are you totally defeated? No. You've still got a couple of aces up your sleeve.

When to Use an Intervention

This is the last chance you have to try to convince your teen to get help voluntarily. It's time to consider using an intervention.

An *intervention* is essentially a carefully planned group confrontation. It involves gathering together as many concerned people as possible, in an atmosphere of love and caring. It is not a time to gang up on the teen and try to make him or her feel guilty. The idea is to confront the teen with the results of his or her drug-abusing behavior. This means giving specific examples of how the teen has hurt those people who love him or her the most. Finally, it's a last opportunity to present the teen with voluntary options for rehabilitation. Usually you only get one shot to make this work, so it's really important to plan the intervention carefully ahead of time. And be sure to leave enough time for rehearsals.

No doubt, you and/or your spouse have tried confronting your drug-abusing teen about his or her behavior before and failed miserably. The problem is that your teen will try to lie to you, shift the blame, or play the two of you off against each other. If this doesn't work, your teen may just refuse to listen and run out of the house, slamming the door.

That's why you need reinforcements.

Enlist Help

The first step in planning an intervention is to enlist the aid of a professional counselor who is experienced in the drug and alcohol abuse field. You can try to get referrals from the telephone book, but it's even better to ask a local juvenile probation officer. They've been through this before and know the most reliable professionals.

To begin the process of putting together an intervention, you want to assemble a group of caring people, people who are all willing to work together for the benefit of the drug-abusing teen. Begin by making a list of all the people you can think of who are important to your child. Try to include someone from every part of his or her life. The immediate family will form the core group. Ideally, this means both parents if they are available. Include any siblings who have been negatively impacted by the drug-abusing behavior and who are old enough to be able to articulate their concerns. Next, consider the extended family—grandparents and any uncles, aunts, or cousins who are aware of the problem and want to help.

Finally, consider the community at large. This includes neighbors, friends of the family, girlfriends (or boyfriends), basketball teammates and employers. Don't forget social service agency providers, members of the clergy, teachers, coaches, school counselors, or other professionals who have been involved with the teen. They should all be invited to attend.

The next step is to contact everyone and arrange for an initial meeting. This is an opportunity to weed out people who are not going to be helpful, such as Uncle Charlie who's always getting drunk at Thanksgiving dinner. Your teen will be quick to pick up on hypocrisy. Another thing to watch out for is the enablers, such as Grandmother Bertha who just "can't believe" that her grandson could do anything wrong. Your teen will be quick to exploit the situation and form an unhealthy alliance, which can undermine the effectiveness of the intervention.

First Meeting

The first meeting of the group is devoted to sharing firsthand information about the teen's alcohol and drug abuse. Just the fact of all these people being assembled in the same room, talking to each other, has an immediate beneficial effect. It irrevocably breaks the denial in the system. That's why experts say that even when an intervention does not achieve the short-term desired result, in the long run it never fails.

At the end of the first meeting, everyone is asked to make a commitment to follow through with the intervention process. For homework, they are each asked to prepare a written statement that they will read to the teen at the intervention. The statement should begin with a declaration of love or affection for the child. A good example is the following: "I'm here tonight out of my love and concern for you. I think the world of you and I'm really worried about some of your recent behavior."

This statement should be followed by a factual description of the teen's drug- or alcohol-related behavior, and how it has caused pain or difficulty for the person speaking. It's important to refrain from condemning the teen or making demeaning remarks. Try to avoid making general statements like, "You're high all the time," which can be challenged by citing exceptions. The following would be a good description from your son or daughter's basketball coach:

> When you miss practice because you're hungover, or come
> to practice high, you hurt the whole team. There's no way
> we can get to the regional finals that way. The team needs
> you to be straight.

The last issue for the first meeting is to agree on the goal of the intervention. Goals may vary depending on circumstance. In this case, however, where serious drug abuse is well documented, the teen has only two options. The first option you offer the teen is to stop using drugs and enter an outpatient treatment program voluntarily. The second option offered to the teen is for him or her to go to a residential treatment facility. That often means a program out of state, which will make it difficult for the teen to run away. Certain states allow teens with drug or emotional problems to be under locked surveillance while other states do not. Find out the legalities of adolescent treatment in your state before you proceed. In either case, it is important that you make arrangements with the treatment facility in advance.

Finally, the teen will be told that noncompliance with either option will result in the parents taking unilateral action. For this to work, parents have to agree ahead of time that they are ready to place the teen in a residential facility, with or without the teen's permission.

Second Meeting

The second meeting of the intervention group is for the purpose of rehearsing the statements and getting feedback from the rest of the group. It is also the time to prepare for all eventualities, such as the following:

What to do if your teen refuses to listen. The intervention simply goes on, with one person speaking at a time. If necessary, participants can get a second chance later, prefacing their remarks by saying, "I'm not sure that you heard me the first time."

What to do if your teen tries to lie or make excuses. The teen is confronted with facts based on firsthand experiences with the participants. You can list events, times, and places.

What to do if your teen yells, screams, or tries to intimidate the participants. The members of the group respond by sitting quietly, not allowing themselves to be drawn into a shouting match. Threats or intimidations are handled by a designated person (usually the professional counselor), who says simply, "There'll be none of that here."

What to do if your teen tries to make others feel guilty. The participants are rehearsed to respond by saying, "That may be true, but we all want you to take responsibility for your behavior."

What to do if the teen tries to leave. Choose the location of the intervention carefully, either a large living room or a downstairs rec room. The biggest, strongest men are assigned to guard any possible exits.

The last issue for this meeting is to set the time and date for the intervention. A careful examination of your child's behavior will show some reliable patterns. For example, you've noticed that your teen always stays out late on Saturday nights and then sleeps in until noon on Sunday. In this case, a good time to arrange for the meeting is early Sunday afternoon.

The Intervention

On the actual day of the intervention, all participants are told to be waiting by the telephone an hour before the event is to begin. The person in charge (the professional counselor) will telephone each participant to confirm that everything is all set or that it has to be postponed for unforeseen reasons. At the given time, your teen is maneuvered to the chosen location. To minimize suspicion, participants should arrive a few at a time, and the selected exit guardians nonchalantly take their stations. When everyone is there the leader says to the teen, "We've all come here today because we care about you and are concerned about your behavior."

The participants then read their statements one at a time. It's a good idea to start with the person who has the most credibility with the teen. The intervention ends with the teen being presented with a written contract to sign. The contract clearly states the options being presented, and the consequences for noncompliance. It's ideal if the teen signs the contract, but not necessary. The participants have been prepared ahead of time for this possibility. Everyone present initials the contract and, one by one, says something to the teen like, "I care about you and want you to turn your life around. I support this contract."

When Treatment Is Not Voluntary

As a parent, you have a couple more options for dealing with a totally uncooperative teen. The first is the controversial practice of sending a teen to an involuntary treatment facility. The second is to get the criminal justice system involved with your teen.

Involuntary Treatment

The first option involves sending your teen off to a distant treatment facility that specializes in behavior modification based on disciplinary tactics. The facilities range from treatment-oriented boarding schools to survivalist programs. Parents can hire a professional escort to transport their teen, against his or her will, to one of these programs.

Pros and Cons

The best approach is to hire an educational consultant or therapist and arrange for an intervention. The resulting behavioral contract includes clear consequences in the event of noncompliance. If the teen is unable to moderate his or her drug use or fails to stay out of trouble, this failure demonstrates a need for more intensive treatment. The adolescent is then offered the option of voluntarily going to the residential facility. Failing that, he or she knows that involuntary placement will result.

Most facilities are fully aware that the manner in which a non-agreeing teen is brought into treatment has a profound affect on the results. They know that teens, manhandled by escorts who are insensitive to the pain and anxiety of their charges, are bound to react with anger and increased resistance to treatment as well.

The majority of escort services hire professionals who take the extra time to talk quietly with the adolescent prior to beginning travel. Many facilities strongly recommend that parents meet their escorted teens at the treatment facility at check-in time. This helps the adolescents understand that they are not being abandoned, and that they still have the love and support of their parents.

The worst approach, much worse than abduction, is intentional deception. When parents deliberately lie to a teen ("Want to come with us on a ski trip?"), they're setting up a situation where trust will be difficult to reestablish.

Programs are located in isolated places in Utah, Montana, South Carolina, Western Samoa and notably, "Tranquility Bay," in Jamaica.

Tranquility Bay

Often involuntary placement is a last resort for parents who are at their wits' end of what to do with an uncooperative and totally out-of-control teen. There have been several publicized cases involving these programs, some seen as successful and others where abuses were noted. One was the notorious Van Blarigan case, which was followed by a number of newspapers. In November 1997, David Van Blarigan (then seventeen years old) was awakened in the middle of the night in Oakland, California and abducted by two burly men hired by his parents. He was eventually transported against his will to the American-owned behavior modification facility called Tranquility Bay on the island of Jamaica. At the airport in Jamaica, he managed to break away and make a telephone call to his close friend and neighbor, saying he wanted to come home. The neighbor, Neil

Aschemeyer, an administrative law judge, contacted David's grandparents. This led to a series of events which resulted in a lengthy court case designed to set him free. Despite their best efforts, however, the grandparents were ultimately unsuccessful in bringing David home. California law is very clear that parents have the right and responsibility to decide what is best for their child. The decision was cheered by a crowd of nearly 100 parents and Teen Help supporters who packed the courtroom.

This case was further explored in a *People* magazine article entitled "Camp Fear" (O'Neill et al. 1998). David's parents had enrolled him in a boot camp–style facility enclosed by high chain-link fences, which specialized in "attitude adjustment." The price tag was $38,000 per year. The program at Tranquility Bay features regimented daily activity and an early-to-bed and early-to-rise philosophy. Teens are required to participate in daily seminars and correspondence classes. The primary focus at the facility is on developing the teen's obedience, sense of respect, and responsibility. There is zero tolerance for breaking the rules. And all behavioral infractions are quickly punished. No outside contact is allowed for the first forty-five days.

Critics call places like Tranquility Bay "hell camps," and say the educational component is a joke. Jay Kay, the owner and operator of Tranquility Bay, pointed out that his program's correspondence curriculum is accredited and supervised by qualified teachers and that medical doctors are available on call. The facility was visited separately by a U.S. embassy official and Jamaican Children's Services authorities. Both gave the place a clean bill of health.

In an interesting postscript, David Van Blarigan wrote a letter from Tranquility Bay to *People* a few weeks after the article about the case appeared in the magazine. The letter read in part:

"I am writing this of my own free will and accord. I love my parents very much, and I am not angry with them for sending me here. . . . I know that my parents made the right decision when they sent me to Tranquility Bay. I was not behaving at home, and I definitely needed something to get me back on track" (Van Blarigan 1998, 6).

Boot Camp Sagas

There have been several reported cases of abusive conditions, such as kids being shackled or hog-tied in these boot camp facilities. There have also been some wrongful death suits.

Stories like these are appalling, and fortunately rare. All in all, these programs are very appealing to desperate families who have an out-of-control teen. Grateful parents call them the best thing that ever happened to their kids.

If you find yourself faced with making the decision to send your son or daughter to one of these programs, be sure to do your homework. Find out all you can about the philosophy, policies, and procedures of the program. Reputable programs will often let you speak with parents of other teens who have gone through them. Find out about how often the officials will be in contact with you about your child's progress and when and how you will hear from your son or daughter. Many programs have a policy of having teens write letters to their parents as treatment progresses. Be sure you will be kept up-to-date on your son or daughter's treatment on a regular and frequent basis. Again, this should not be a first choice but should be reserved for severe situations where you are deeply concerned that no other option will work and that your child's life is in danger.

Law and Order

It's every parent's worst nightmare. The telephone rings, and when you answer it, an official-sounding voice says, "Mrs. Jones?"

"Yes it is."

"This is Captain Belson, we have your son Billy down here at police headquarters. We've arrested him for possession of cocaine. He was also smoking marijuana when we caught him."

Most parents dread the thought of being faced with this scenario. The idea of your son or daughter being arrested and taken into custody can be frightening. But for an out-of-control teen who won't cooperate with your rules or consequences, involvement with the juvenile justice system can feel like a lifesaver. Once your teen is in the system, he or she will have to answer to a higher authority. If your teen doesn't comply with court orders, he or she can be taken into custody again. This is frequently a strong deterrent.

You also have the option of trying to get your teen into the system. If you know your son or daughter is involved in criminal activity, above and beyond drug use, you can bring it to the attention of the police. Getting your child arrested can be a difficult action to take, but it is one that many parents and teens have been grateful for in the end.

Once a teen is arrested, he or she may either spend time in juvenile hall or be released to a parent while awaiting a court date. Once charges are filed, the teen will be assigned a public defender, or you can hire an attorney to represent your child. When your teen appears in court, there may be different options available. What you want to push for is treatment and not jail time. If there is a juvenile drug court in your county, you can request that the case be transferred to that court if it has not already been done. Usually the charge has to involve drugs or alcohol to be referred to drug court. But even if the charge is for another crime, making a strong point about your child's use of drugs or alcohol may get you the help you are seeking.

Juvenile Drug Court

As of June 2001, there were 167 juvenile drug courts in 46 states. And an additional 113 JDCs are in the planning stage. Since the inception of the JDC program, over 12,000 juveniles have enrolled. There are about 4,500 current participants and over 4,000 graduates. This translates into an impressive 68 percent retention rate.

The goal of juvenile drug court is to help the juvenile break his or her pattern of alcohol or drug abuse and stop the negative behaviors that go along with it. Successful completion of the juvenile drug court program may result in early termination of probation. The main characteristics of juvenile drug court are

- intense supervision by the court

- frequent drug testing

- positive consequences (rewards) for compliant behavior

- swift negative consequences for noncompliant behavior

- peer support

Juvenile drug courts have a number of key components.

They integrate treatment services with the juvenile justice system. JDCs provide access to a continuum of alcohol, drug, and related treatment and rehabilitation services. The degree of jail time and in-custody treatment may vary, depending on the nature of the offense and the degree of substance abuse.

They use a non-adversarial approach. Prosecution and defense counsel work together to negotiate win-win solutions, while protecting participants' due process rights.

They stress early intervention. Eligible participants are identified quickly and promptly. Usually participants meet with a probation officer within twenty-four hours of arrest.

They have intense court involvement. Teens must initially make weekly court appearances. There are only two ways to end court involvement: graduation from the program or sentencing to jail.

Abstinence is monitored by frequent and random drug testing. For the first positive (dirty) drug test, the probation officer has the discretion to impose a sanction (e.g., house arrest). The second relapse results in up to five days in juvenile hall. After a third positive drug test the juvenile is usually placed in a residential treatment facility. These sanctions may vary from state to state.

Parent involvement is mandatory. This may mean transporting the juvenile to treatment sessions or holding regular family meetings. Often it means attendance at Al-Anon meetings or parenting classes.

Case Histories

The following case histories are composites drawn from a number of actual cases and developed with the help of a juvenile drug court probation officer who works in California. These case histories are presented in the style of probation reports.

Sharonda's Story: A Favorable Outcome

Sharonda, a fourteen-year-old female, was placed on juvenile probation for possession of methamphetamine. She was observed by a teacher, and caught with a small bindle of crank at the junior high school during recess. As a result of the offense, the court set a maximum confinement time of one year. She was placed in the juvenile drug court program and ordered to make regular court appearances; therapeutic detention in the juvenile hall was stayed, pending further disposition. She was also assigned a drug court judge who would monitor her compliance and hold her accountable for any violations. Success, as demonstrated by negative drug tests, would be rewarded by fewer court appearances and reduced probation time.

When Sharonda entered the juvenile justice system she had been living with her mother, a single parent, in a motel room. Sharonda's non-biological father, who had raised her since age three, had recently separated from her mother and was living with friends. Sharonda's biological father had recently reappeared, and contact between them had just begun to take place. Her mother was unemployed, had severe financial problems, and had a significant alcohol and drug problem of her own. Sharonda received little or no supervision within the home and was frequently absent from the alternative school she was attending. She was a special education student with multiple learning disabilities.

Sharonda's drug/alcohol history had begun at age eleven with alcohol. She started to smoke marijuana during the sixth grade and began experimenting with methamphetamine two years later. Additional complicating factors included a history of bulimia, self-mutilation, and suicide attempts. There was also indication of sexual molestation by a family acquaintance, but the matter had never been formally investigated.

A number of interventions took place with Sharonda and her family. Working across systems, several agencies became involved to address her multiple needs. The court arranged for Sharonda to get a court advocate, a trained volunteer who would serve as an appropriate adult role model and provide ongoing support. Administrators of Sharonda's treatment program, her probation officer, and the court all attempted to intervene with the mother. Sharonda's mother refused treatment, however, and later abandoned her daughter. When Sharonda had an occasional positive drug test, she was held accountable with appropriate sanctions.

Sharonda's biological father was encouraged to reenter his daughter's life. He responded by providing transportation, as well as taking responsibility for her primary needs such as medical and dental coverage. The probation officer set up multiple meetings with the school and communication links were established between school, home, and probation. When Sharonda made the transition to high school, her probation officer advocated for additional educational support through a tutoring program and special education classes.

A mental health evaluation had been ordered by the court and completed. While major mental health problems were ruled out, it was clear that Sharonda was experiencing significant emotional distress. She was referred to a psychotherapist. Sharonda later filed a police report regarding the alleged molestation. She felt more empowered by her work with the authorities. As a result, she became eligible for the Victim Witness program, a state-funded program for victims or witnesses of violent crimes; the program paid for long-term therapy.

Sharonda's residence was changed to her biological father's home. He provided a stable environment while her other needs were being addressed. She attended an outpatient program, sometimes accompanied by both her fathers. Over time Sharonda began to achieve some success. She received an award for improvement at school and became a member of the basketball team. She also did volunteer work with younger children.

Sharonda graduated from outpatient treatment and followed her aftercare plan, which included attending NA meetings and seeing her sponsor. She got a part-time job and started doing chores around the house. Her biological father, recognizing his need for support in his new role as a parent, began attending parent education classes. The probation officer arranged for a meeting with the family's therapist and both fathers. This was to address the long-term issue of Sharonda's attempt to play one parent against the other. The fathers were able to learn to communicate and cooperate, removing a block to Sharonda's success.

Sharonda graduated from high school with a GPA of 3.8 around the same time she graduated from drug court. A one-year follow-up, post probation, found her continuing to do well in all areas. The occasional challenges that had occurred were handled within the family.

What Worked in This Case?

1. There was at least one parent (actually two in this case) who cared about the teen and were actively involved in her recovery.

2. The young woman had incredible internal strength and resiliency. And she was motivated to do well. She used available support systems which were offered by the court.

3. All the professionals involved in multiple systems (court, probation, therapists, police department, special education personnel) coordinated their efforts and worked well together.

4. Probation was used appropriately to back up the parent as needed. The probation officer provided ongoing close supervision (including random search of the minor's belongings), drug testing, and monitoring school attendance.

5. Regular court hearings held before the same judge served as a continual reminder to Sharonda that she would be held accountable for her actions.

Zeke's Story: Dealing with Denial

Ezekiel (Zeke), a seventeen-year-old male, was placed on juvenile probation as a result of possession of cocaine. When arrested, he was under the influence of cocaine and driving without a license. He had one prior police referral involving cocaine. Zeke was sentenced to the maximum confinement time of three years. He was placed on juvenile probation with all standard conditions; therapeutic detention time was stayed pending further disposition, and he was placed in the juvenile drug court.

Zeke's family history was marked by chaos and instability. His mother had a serious drug problem that had resulted in constant upheaval. He had never had any contact with his father. At the time he was placed on probation he was living with his grandmother. She was a kind woman but overwhelmed by the responsibility of caring for a number of grandchildren. She was also the primary caregiver for a critically ill son.

When Zeke was interviewed, he reported a three-year history of regular marijuana use and at least a year of cocaine abuse. Oddly, he did not see himself as having a drug problem. His attendance at school was poor, and he was lacking in high school credits.

Zeke had an immediate positive response to probation. He stated that he knew he needed to be arrested and wanted to change his life. Improvements were noted in both attitude and behavior. He applied to a work-study program and began attending church with his family. He also began attending outpatient treatment in a social model program, four days a week. There he received tutoring support, and was enrolled in a temporary school program. He was also put on a waiting list for a highly structured job training/GED program, which could lead to a good union job. Weekly random drug tests all came up clean.

Zeke bonded quickly with many of the professionals he came to know. He presented himself as polite and mild mannered, always knowing the right thing to say. He always showed up on time, eager to learn. He was never a problem or disruptive. In each program he was considered a top student and a role model.

Approximately three months into his probationary period, Zeke was arrested for a violent and possibly drug-related offense. The circumstances were highly suspicious, but charges were later dropped. All the professionals working with him at the time of his arrest were shocked, and found the allegations to be completely out of character with what they had observed about him. As a result, he was given many hours of one-on-one counseling. Zeke continued with his treatment, school, and job programs and again achieved the same high level of success.

A probation officer searched his room and belongings on a random basis, always coming up empty. Routine random drug tests also tested negative for drugs. The court rewarded his positive behavior with praise, raised his curfew, and even gave him gift certificates to a local record store.

Zeke, however, had been living a double life. And eventually it caught up with him. Another five months went by uneventfully, but then Zeke was arrested again, this time on a felony drug sales charge which was sustained. He was terminated from juvenile drug court and served several months in juvenile hall as a result. After he got out of detention, he was referred to a residential drug program.

What Went Wrong in this Case?

1. Zeke's home situation contained too many people with multiple needs, and the responsible adult was overwhelmed with demands.

2. The parent (grandparent in this case) was an enabler. She was always pleasant and never reported any wrongdoings although she most likely was aware of such activities.

3. The teen was in denial about his drug use, and he was never directly confronted about it. He was never really willing to change.

4. The treatment program did not have a family therapy component.

5. Sociopathic skills that Zeke had developed ultimately undermined his chance for recovery. He was able to fool the professionals and other helpers, to his own detriment.

What can you learn from these two stories? On the face of it, Zeke seemed ideally suited to become the poster child for success in juvenile drug court, while Sharonda, with multiple strikes against her, including an eating disorder, self-mutilation, a suicide attempt, and history of molestation, seemed destined for failure. Why did one child fail and the other succeed?

One critical element emerges: parental involvement and cooperation. Zeke's grandmother was someone who really was doing the best she could under overwhelming conditions. And yet, it was her inability to cooperate with probation which set the stage for Zeke's failure. She was the one who was in the best position to observe Zeke's behavior and report it to probation.

Sharonda's story demonstrates the other side of the coin. A previously absent father returns and gets involved with his daughter. Sharonda ends up with not one but two caring fathers who learn to work together, and cooperate fully with probation.

Hopefully, you will have the time and energy to focus on your teenager's needs. Your involvement is crucial.

Seelah's Story: A Bumpy Road

Thirteen-year-old female, Seelah, was placed on juvenile probation for felony possession of cocaine. She was arrested at her home where she was also found to be under the influence of cocaine, subsequent to a telephone tip from her parents. The maximum confinement time set by the juvenile drug court was three years, but she was placed on probation with standard drug and alcohol, as well as gang, conditions. Therapeutic detention time in juvenile hall was imposed but stayed pending further disposition.

Prior to being placed on probation, Seelah was already well known to the police department as a chronic runaway and school truant. She was also known for her involvement in gang activity. Her parents had been frustrated for some time and had little or no control over her behavior. Seelah's drug use reportedly began at age eleven and included marijuana, alcohol, crank, and cocaine. Seelah primarily associated with older friends and appeared to be sexually active. Her parents had previously attempted to get help through a counseling program, and continued to attend sessions even after their daughter dropped out.

Juvenile drug court provided the teen with a high degree of structure. Seelah was initially placed under house arrest and subject to intense supervision, including random urine testing. Subsequently, she received a complete drug and alcohol assessment and was referred to outpatient treatment. Within a week, she violated the terms of her probation by meeting with gang members and using drugs. She was placed in juvenile hall and put on a waiting list for a gang intervention program.

Seelah exhibited a brief period of success after this but subsequently violated the terms of her probation again. This time she was introduced to the gang program and began attendance while in custody. Upon her release she was placed in a highly structured school program and attended outpatient treatment and the gang program concurrently. Her parents attended a parent education program, and Seelah began to succeed in school.

A few months later, however, she ran away from home again and put herself in a very high-risk situation involving drugs, sexual activity, and violence. When Seelah was finally located, she was placed under arrest and put in the secure custody of juvenile hall. It was obvious that she could no longer be safely maintained at home. Despite great effort and multiple therapeutic interventions, all outpatient treatment attempts had failed. Seelah was clearly in need of a higher level of care.

Seelah received a mental health evaluation and after an interview with a drug-abuse counselor, was mandated to a long-term residential treatment facility. After an initial period of resistance there, she gradually came out of her shell and began to address her personal issues. The program provided support and therapy which enabled her to confront her history of trauma, which included sexual abuse and rape. Seelah's parents consistently attended family therapy sessions and were supportive of treatment professionals. Over time, Seelah began to blossom. Eighteen months later, she was a strong, assertive young woman. She was able to express her feelings appropriately and set boundaries with her peers and adults.

After her graduation from the residential program, the probation officer continued to supervise her progress. Seelah attended both NA and aftercare meetings, forming a healthy support network. She finished her educational program and received a G.E.D. A year post treatment, and off probation, Seelah was clean and sober, with no further arrests.

What Worked in This Case?

1. Both parents were actively involved in the rehabilitation process. They consistently attended family education meetings and family therapy sessions.

2. The parents were willing to be proactive. They took responsibility for getting help for their daughter, even if it meant calling the police and having her arrested.

3. Juvenile drug court and the probation officer consistently applied appropriate sanctions for the teen's behavior.

4. When lower level treatment interventions failed, the probation officer was able to mandate a higher level of care.

If your son or daughter should become involved with the law, hopefully you can take advantage of the juvenile drug court system. This program can be a helpful ally in your attempts to get your teen to comply with your rules and limits and to enroll them in a treatment program. Your child's behavior will be closely monitored, leaving him or her little room to get back into negative and harmful situations.

If you are not lucky enough to have a juvenile drug court in your community, don't give up hope. In most cases, you can arrange for similar conditions with the juvenile justice system and local probation officers. It just means that you have to do more work to make it happen.

CHAPTER 10

Hope

A lesson from the Greek myth, Pandora's Box, can keep us going in the face of negativity and crisis. The myth tells the story of how Pandora was sent by Zeus to the gods, Prometheus and Epimetheus, as punishment for stealing fire from heaven and giving it to man. Zeus gave Pandora a jar and told her not to open it under any circumstances. But Pandora couldn't contain her curiosity, and she removed the lid of the jar, allowing all kinds of evil and illness to escape and spread across the earth. Pandora tried to replace the lid but couldn't. Everything escaped from the jar with the exception of Hope, which lay at the bottom. And so it is that no matter what kind of evil and illnesses are around us, Hope has not left us entirely.

Your teen is tampering with his or her own jar of illness and evil when experimenting with drugs and alcohol. And the longer the contents are swarming around, the more deeply in trouble your teen will become. But there is still hope available. You just have to tap into what and where hope lies for your teen.

Hope is a hard thing to hold on to when struggling with so many difficult issues. But hope does exist in even the most disastrous of circumstances.

Have Patience and Courage

Remain hopeful about your teen by developing a great deal of patience and an even greater amount of courage. Having faith that your teen's and family's troubles can be resolved means that you'll have to hang in there. And to stay in this struggle is hard work on many levels. You will need time, energy, and support to help you through. You will have to confront many losses, disillusionment, and often despair.

Helping your teen recover from drug and alcohol use, especially if you are dealing with a teen who is abusing or dependent, is a long process. Most of the time, there is no quick fix that will make the problem go away. There will be many twists and turns, some disappointments, and frequently a few failures for your family. The problems of teen substance abuse are multifaceted. As you deal with each of the issues, you will have to keep your sights on the goals you want to reach for both your teen and family. You will have to accept that you'll make mistakes and that you'll have to try new or different methods or strategies. You will have to accept that your teen will make mistakes too, sometimes taking two steps forward and one step back. You might even find that your teen seems to be moving backward or sideways with little progress at all. The path to health and recovery is not usually a straight and easy one. Patience will be an essential tool as you work through the difficulties.

This is where courage comes into play. Hanging in there not only means you believe the situation can improve, it means facing emotions, family dynamics, or truths about yourself that you may have been avoiding. And after confronting those realities, you'll have to do something about them. Change will be critical for you and your teen to reach a successful outcome. And if you believe that, then you have to be willing to do what it takes to make change happen.

Many parents say that they want to confront the issues that plague their family and make changes. But wanting to do this and really doing the hard work to make it happen are two very different things. You'll have to swallow your pride at times, reach out and let others help you, and be open to new possibilities. You'll have to trust others and trust the process, sometimes going on blind faith that the suggestions for change are worthwhile. Your family will have to try new things and learn about each other in different ways. For many parents, this idea is overwhelming and can bring up feelings of fear and doubt. Finding the courage to make lasting change may not come easily and will take much of your focus.

Some parents find that they can't take the stress that focusing on themselves and their family creates. They find it easier to give up the struggle rather than fight for their teen. It's not that they don't love their child, or lack a sincere desire to help them, but they get caught up in the enormity of the situation and give up. They might decide to just let their child continue using. Or they may send their son or daughter off to live with a relative or to a long-term treatment program that doesn't require parental involvement. These parents are not necessarily giving up on their teen, but may be too fearful, lacking the courage to persevere.

If this sounds like something you're experiencing, you may not have found the right support to help you with the struggle. It's hard to go it alone and keep a perspective on where you're going and what you're trying to achieve. Professionals, as well as family and friends, can help you stay on task and keep up the hard work.

You may feel the loss of your dreams for your son or daughter, which can bring on disillusionment or despair. Parents often talk about having to give up on plans that they thought were already set in motion. If your son had potential to excel in a sport or on a musical instrument but his commitment has been derailed by his drug use, you may be quite disappointed. If you were planning on college for your daughter, only to discover that her grades are barely passing and that she might not even graduate from high school, you may be ready to throw in the towel.

You may even feel that your ideal of who and what your family was all about has been shattered. You might question your parenting, or your capacity to do what's right. These can send you into feelings of true despair. We know it sounds a bit crazy, but until you face all of these feelings and acknowledge that they're there, you won't be able to get to the place of hope we're talking about. If you deal with these feelings head on, getting support and guidance along the way, you will have a truer picture of where things might be going. This will help you stay on course with your teen.

How to Measure Success

For many parents, there comes a time when they don't feel any faith that things will improve. The situation feels bleak and hopeless. This is a time when many parents feel like giving up. They've tried new approaches at home, they've monitored behavior, made changes for their teen, even enrolled him or her in a treatment program. And still the drug and alcohol use continues.

It's important to begin with realistic expectations of success for your teen. If your expectations are unrealistic, you'll find it harder to remain patient and keep your hope alive. Putting your teen's drug use in context and comparing it to what we know about teen recovery from drug and alcohol use and abuse is a useful place for you to start.

Outcome studies on people entering substance treatment programs are in short supply. What information is available is mostly anecdotal and collected by individual programs. This information suggests that the average addicted person goes through multiple treatment attempts before getting clean and sober. The first attempt at recovery is not always successful. For people who have entered a treatment program, generally between one-third to one-half of those individuals are considered successful (Hubbard 2001). The success rate is a little lower for teens.

But how do you measure success? Programs measure success in many different ways. For some, success means that a client completely stops using for a period of time. It can mean that clients are clean and sober at the end of treatment, or that they're still not using one year or more after treatment ends. For other programs, success may mean that a client is still using but no longer breaks the law in order to do so. Success is then measured by information on whether people are now using "the system," or if they're functioning on their own and becoming a taxpayer and not a tax taker.

Each program and each person has to be looked at separately. Some people will have a 100 percent success rate on their very first try at treatment. Others may never be successful at getting clean and sober, living a life of addiction until their death.

For teens who have not hit bottom and are not voluntarily seeking treatment, a successful first treatment attempt is not always possible. We find that the earlier the problem is addressed, the higher the success rates. Your teen may require more treatment and tougher bottom lines, which may require some difficult decisions on your part. The key is that you've got to hang in there because it's worth it in the end.

The following stories about real teens illustrate how success can be measured.

Darren's Story

Darren entered treatment in a residential program when he was seventeen. He came from an upper-middle class background with many privileges and opportunities. He'd been smoking marijuana since he was thirteen, and by the time he was sixteen, he was shooting heroin. He was the only one of his drug-using friends doing heroin. A friend's older brother had introduced him to it.

Darren did well in treatment. He worked hard on his own recovery, used family therapy sessions to deal with issues he had at home, and was helpful to other teens in treatment with him. But he was honest about his love for heroin and his reluctance to give it up.

He left treatment at eighteen and went back out, eventually using heroin daily. His addiction continued for three more years, taking him to seedy back alleys and removing him completely from contact with his family. His parents were devastated by his continued use, but always tried to find out where he was and how he was doing. They wouldn't let him move back home while he was still using, but they continued to let him know that their love for him was always there, and that when he was ready to help himself, they'd be there to support him. It wasn't until he landed in another city across the country that he met someone who told him about a treatment program that might work for him. He went into treatment soon afterwards. Later he remarked that although he hadn't been ready to get clean when he was in treatment at seventeen, the therapy, the classes, and the exposure to recovery concepts had planted a seed in him. He carried that seed with him for the next three years, always knowing that there was something else available to him besides his addiction. When he was ready for treatment, he knew what to do. He asked his parents for their support and they agreed to pay for the treatment program. The reunion with his family after six months of treatment was bittersweet. They'd lost contact for years and had many issues to work through as a family, but they were grateful that Darren had found a way back to health and recovery.

If Darren's family had given up on him and refused to help him get into treatment again, he might never have received the help he needed and deserved. Similarly, he might never have been helped if they had caved in to Darren's demands to let him use but still live at home. Darren's family remained hopeful by maintaining strong family ties, continuing attendance at support groups for family members of addicts, and by listening to the suggestions of others who had gone through similar problems.

Krista's Story

Hope and success come in different forms. You won't always be able to measure success immediately. And the successes you achieve may not always be the ones you originally set out to accomplish. Often, there will be changes that happen to your family that you didn't expect.

Krista, a sixteen-year-old, had been trying to stop using marijuana for over a year. Her father was an alcoholic and came from a family with an extensive history of alcoholism. Her mother did not have an alcohol problem, but she too had a family history of alcoholism and grew up with an alcoholic father. Krista's older brother was also using drugs, both marijuana and amphetamines.

Krista was in two different outpatient treatment programs over the course of a year but couldn't stay away from drug-using friends and the drugs they provided. She and her family struggled with the addiction that permeated her family. During this time, her father addressed his alcoholism, her mother's co-dependency issues became a focus of treatment, and her older brother got into a treatment program. But Krista continued to feel compelled to smoke marijuana regularly. She was angry with the program's staff because with all the information she had gained through treatment, she couldn't ignore what her use was doing to her. She frequently exclaimed that treatment was a "buzz kill" and had ruined her high. She could no longer use drugs and deny the problems using caused her and her family. She couldn't just numb herself with drugs anymore.

Krista eventually agreed to go to a residential treatment program where she remained for three months. Before she left for the program, her father made a decision to quit drinking and began attending a support group twice a week. Krista's mother went to a codependents support group and worked on her enabling behaviors. After treatment, her older brother remained clean and sober and joined the Peace Corps to help others in another country. The family was getting help, both individually and as a family unit. They were happier and healthier than they had ever been.

Krista successfully completed treatment after three months and was a role model for many of the other teens in the program. She was nearly eighteen years of age and decided to move out with a couple of friends, get a job, and try recovery on her own for a while. Within a month, Krista began smoking marijuana again. She continued to struggle with what that meant for her and her future. But entrance into treatment two years earlier had set her family on a new course that permitted lasting changes for every one of them. Krista's dad remained sober. Her mother and father had a new relationship, where they supported one another and were more available to support their kids. After returning from the Peace Corps, her brother started college and became engaged to a woman with no history of addiction in her family.

The family supported Krista's efforts to change her life. Krista knew she had to give up her using friends and the lifestyle they led. She still smoked marijuana, but not daily and not to the point where it rendered her helpless to support herself.

Is Krista's a success story? Is there hope when you read these words? Yes, perhaps Krista could be further along on the road to health. But she and her family have grown in many positive ways. They are attempting to break the cycle of addiction that has plagued their family for generations.

When the focus was solely on how to get Krista to change, no one thought about how there might be hope for the family as a whole and for each family member individually. Krista's family members have become remarkable role models, which, in turn, could help Krista beat her own substance abuse.

What Sobriety Can Bring

Many people who enter treatment do not expect the many changes that come with sobriety. Adults in treatment have commented that they feel *lucky*, if you can believe it, to have had an addiction and to have opportunities to make changes in all aspects of their lives. The devastation that their addiction created served as a catalyst to address all sorts of issues that surrounded their use. They've discovered benefits to treatment and sobriety that go way beyond stopping their use of alcohol or drugs.

Many addicts faced early traumas or great difficulties in their childhood that contributed to their use of substances. As we've discussed, using drugs is a way to numb out or escape from painful feelings.

Once they gain those tools that recovery offers and feel the support of a twelve-step or recovery program, many people are open to tackling painful histories and working through long-standing problems. In this case, getting clean and sober brings more than a healthier lifestyle because of no drinking or drugging. Recovery also means living a richer, fuller, happier life, with new ways of dealing with yourself and with the people around you.

Jasmine's Story

Jasmine was a fifteen-year-old girl when she was arrested for possession of alcohol and marijuana. She also used psychedelic drugs regularly but didn't have any with her at the time of her arrest.

Jasmine's life had not been easy. Her parents were divorced and she had a distant relationship with her father and his new family. When Jasmine visited her father, she and her stepmother would have screaming matches, which usually resulted in Jasmine being sent back home to her mother. Jasmine's mother had a full-time job to help with their support and was not home until after dinner every day.

There had been other incidents involving drugs or alcohol in the year before Jasmine's arrest, including suspension from school for being drunk. The police had stopped Jasmine and her friends on other occasions as well but had just sent the kids on their way after warning them about being drunk in public. She hid her use from her mother, who had no idea until her arrest about Jasmine's involvement with drugs or alcohol.

The next year and a half were a nightmare for the family. Not much happened to Jasmine at her court hearing other than a fine and two weekends of community service, along with an admonishment not to use anymore, but Jasmine was determined to do just the opposite. She began using drugs more frequently, cutting school and getting high on a daily basis. She dropped her interest in the piano and her dream of becoming a singer-songwriter. She cared about little else besides getting high. Her mother pleaded with Jasmine to stop using. She tried bribing her with gifts, took her to psychotherapy, and tried grounding her for breaking the rules. None of this did any good. Jasmine's relationship with her mother deteriorated into worse fights than she'd had with her stepmother. Jasmine would regularly threaten to hit her mother or to commit suicide if her mother didn't leave her alone. Her mom felt like she was being held hostage in her own home.

Jasmine's parents were unable to see eye to eye on what to do about Jasmine's drug use, and in spite of the difficulties with her dad's new family, Jasmine went to live with them. The fights with her stepmother increased as her father spent more time away on business trips. Jasmine was left on her own much of the time, which allowed her to abuse drugs and cut school any time she liked. There wasn't much her mother could do to intervene.

Almost one year after her first arrest, Jasmine was arrested again for possession of marijuana. It may have been the best thing that happened to her. This time Jasmine's father decided that he, too, had had enough of her drug abuse, and both parents went to court to try to convince the judge to give Jasmine more than a fine or community service. Fortunately, this judge himself had raised a drug-abusing teen and knew that serious intervention was the best course of action. Jasmine was placed in a residential treatment program and then transferred to a therapeutic boarding school.

By the time Jasmine graduated from high school, she had made a remarkable turnaround. She had been clean and sober for two years. She went from failing all her classes to passing with honors. She resumed her piano lessons and began taking voice lessons, to help her with a career in the music industry.

Jasmine not only cleaned up her drug problem; she also addressed many other issues. She dealt with the painful feelings that surrounded her parents' divorce and her feelings of being abandoned by her father. She once again became respectful and honest, and she developed a new moral and spiritual outlook on life. She established a deeply moral value system that included the immense importance of family. She and her mother became close again. Jasmine and her father worked on their relationship. She began a different kind of relationship with his new wife and their kids. She became a mentor to her younger half-siblings, discussing the perils of drug use. Had she not been removed from her negative environment, she never would have worked on these issues.

Negative behaviors go hand in hand with using. It's hard to keep doing something that is bad for you without having to resort to lying, hiding, and ignoring loved ones. There's usually a cycle of using and other negative behaviors, feeling guilty about what you've done, not wanting to face it, and using to cover up the feelings, which just starts the cycle all over again. Often, even when they recognize the negative way they're behaving, people can't stop the behaviors while they're still using. It isn't until they get clean and sober that they're able to act differently. They no longer have to lie, or steal, or stay away from family. They can stop being selfish, short-tempered, or suspicious of what others think. Often people may start out on their path to recovery just to get rid of their use of substances, but they end up making unexpected changes that delight them and those who care about them. And often those changes are lifelong ones that stay with them even if they backslide into using again.

Be Prepared for Relapse

Addiction is a relapsing condition. Let's just say that up front. If it were an easy problem to get over, there would be no need for drug treatment programs, twelve-step programs or the like. Remember how we referred to the desire of so many people to alter their consciousness? From children swinging around to get that dizzy feeling to so many of the world's cultures using substances to change their perceptions, the compulsion to change our consciousness is very deeply ingrained. And let's not pretend that there aren't some fun things about those kinds of feelings. People wouldn't keep using if they didn't like certain aspects of the high. The desire to use, remembering the good times and feelings you had while using, remains very strong for most people for a long period of time.

It's no wonder then, that even when people do get clean and sober—even when they are grateful for the changes their recovery from addiction has done for their lives—they continue to have a strong desire to use again. Often, once people have achieved a period of sobriety, and they have their lives more under control, they will convince themselves that they can handle using again—in moderation, of course. For most addicts, this is not possible. Using in moderation quickly returns them to a pattern of using that was unhealthy and extreme.

Some treatment programs make a distinction between a "slip," a onetime use of substances again after a period of sobriety, and a full-blown relapse, a return to previous patterns of use. There is hope for those folks who can get back on track after realizing they made a mistake, can admit the mistake to themselves and to others, and begin the necessary steps to keep them sober in the future. But there is even hope for those who drop back into their addiction. The other life changes we mentioned that result from recovery can often serve as a catalyst to getting back into treatment.

Relapse can be a learning experience for many people once they do get back into living a life of recovery. People can learn from their mistakes. A relapse can be a deterrent for future relapses. Someone who has relapsed can share his or her experience with others who might be toying with using again. We've seen this method work.

Special Hope for Adolescents

The large majority of teens who try drugs and alcohol do not go on to become regular users or abusers. In comparison to the number of teens who will try alcohol, marijuana, and cigarettes, the number whose use becomes problematic is relatively small. As we hope you've learned from this book, this fact doesn't mean that you should ignore your teen's use or avoid discussing with your teen the risks of using. If you are faced with a teen who is experimenting or even using regularly, you may be able to avoid further problems with abuse by addressing the use now.

For teens who are abusing or addicted, there is still hope to turn their lives around because they are still adolescents. The fact that they are young, and that their abuse or addiction is relatively new compared to most adults who try recovery, makes their chances for a successful recovery relatively good. Certainly someone using for fewer than three to five years will have an easier time getting clean, in most cases, than someone who has a thirty-year history of addiction. Another reason for hope is that the lives of most abusing or addicted teens have not been completely shattered. Compared with the experience of adults, it will take less time and effort to rebuild their lives. And adolescents have more time and chances to make something different happen for themselves than do most adults leaving treatment.

When drug-abusing teens attend twelve-step meetings, it is common to hear adults in attendance exclaim how pleased they are to see teens getting clean so early on in their lives. They often express hope for the teens, knowing that if they themselves had entered treatment as teens, their lives would be so much better.

Prevention Techniques

You can do a lot to help your teen avoid using drugs. The more you talk with your teen about drugs and alcohol in an honest, open, and nonjudgmental fashion, the more your teen will talk to you too. Open communication channels will make it easier to deal with a drug problem should one arise. Listen as much as, if not more than, you talk. Ask your teen's opinions on drinking and drug use. Ask how your teen feels about other kids who are using. Establish your rules clearly and let your teen know what will happen if you discover there is ongoing use. Give your son or daughter a few outs to use with peers when confronted with drug use: "My parents randomly drug test me now that they heard I tried weed, so I can't join you guys." Or, "I've got addiction in my family, so I've got to stay away from even drinking a little." Such statements can help your teen in situations where drugs and alcohol are present. And assume that your teen will be in such situations in your discussions with him or her. Let's face it. Your teen is going to be around drugs and alcohol. Establish a policy on what your teen can do in a situation where drugs and alcohol are being used: "Call me and I promise there will be no questions asked about who and why. I'll just come pick you up, so you don't have to get into a car with a bunch of drunk kids."

Remember that your own habits are a model for how your teen deals with drugs and alcohol. Using substances in moderation, if at all, will serve as an example to your teen. Even behaviors that have nothing to do with your use of substances can affect your teen's use. If you are always dieting or eating excessively and preoccupied with weight, or if you chain-smoke, you're communicating a lack of respect for your body and others' health. If you drive too fast and cut off other drivers when you're in a hurry, you're sending a message about irresponsible behavior and risk taking.

Finally, encourage your teen's involvement in positive interests. Sports, music, art, school clubs, and volunteer work or a paid job are great opportunities for your son or daughter to develop responsibility and a sense of self-worth. These interests can be a way to direct your teen's energy toward something positive. Such activities can help your teen become more confident, creative, and involved in the community.

Partners in Prevention

An essential component of your response to your teen's use of drugs and alcohol are the partnerships you establish in your community. If you don't already have a relationship with your teen's school, parent-teacher organizations, and community groups, try to get that started. You cannot do this alone. Although these groups may not specifically center around adolescent use of drugs and alcohol, they can be powerful allies in addressing these critical problems. The more support and backup you have for your policies, the better. Make sure these partners are aware of programs in your community that are available for teens at all stages of use. Find out which therapists, pediatricians, and other health professionals have expertise in adolescent substance abuse and find ways to use them as resources for you and other parents.

Contact your local law enforcement agencies to get their involvement. Too many police and sheriff departments ignore minor drug or alcohol offenses and wait until there are major problems before intervening. It seems that especially with offenses involving alcohol, a substance legal for adults, the police may take a hands-off approach unless the offense involves drinking and driving.

Encourage your teen to form positive relationships with other adults. Coaches, youth ministers, older siblings or other family members, and parents of friends are great resources for teens to utilize. If they feel like they can talk to other adults when they're less comfortable talking to their parents, they'll be able to share and confide in someone who can give them a positive perspective.

Probably your best partners in preventing drug problems are other parents. Get to know the parents of your teen's friends. As your children are getting older, more mobile, and more independent, you probably don't have the same contact with other parents that you did when your kids were younger. But other parents can be real allies in your effort to keep your teen drug free. Share your policies on drug and alcohol use with them. Establish shared expectations about curfew, unchaperoned parties, and places teens may go.

You may want to take advantage of parent support groups or parenting classes available through a community organization. First of all, it helps to know there are other parents dealing with similar issues. Secondly, it can be insightful to hear how other parents deal with their teen. Get involved on as many levels of support as you can. Many communities have groups for parents specifically dealing with teen drug and alcohol use.

There are also twelve-step and other substance-abuse support groups with an emphasis on parents dealing with their child's use of substances. In addition to Al-Anon, which is a spin-off organization of Alcoholics Anonymous, there are Narcotics Anonymous and Nar-Anon. In many communities, Al-Anon and Nar-Anon have support meetings specifically for parents of abusing teens and young adults. We have already mentioned TOUGHLOVE (see chapter 8). Your community may have additional groups available to you. Substance-abuse treatment programs in your area that focus on adolescents will also have resources for parents.

It's Up to You

We're asking a lot of you. We recognize that the amount of time, energy, and money involved may be enormous. We acknowledge that we're asking you to stretch yourself in ways you may have never considered. You may be resistant or doubtful that the material in the book pertains to your child or will be useful to you.

We wouldn't be making these suggestions if we weren't positive that they are essential in helping you to help your teen. After years of experience and contact with hundreds of families, we believe the information we provide and the methods we suggest are the best course of action for you to take. But you know your child and you know yourself better than anyone. You have to do what feels right. You have to assess what you and your family can manage. We invite you to be open to our suggestions and use our guidelines in any way that is useful. Check out our suggestions with other parents who have dealt with an abusing teen. Ask health care professionals about the information we've provided.

What we're mainly emphasizing is that you do *something*. We want you to take action and do the hard work necessary to get your teen off of drugs and alcohol or to prevent your teen from ever using or abusing drugs or alcohol. It's so worth it because we're talking about your child, our world's most important future asset. It's up to you.

APPENDIX A

Street Slang

What follows is based primarily on a data base originally created by one of authors in the Haight Ashbury district of San Francisco in 1980. This has been supplemented and updated by a national survey undertaken early in 2002, with the help of Daytop in New York City, Samaritan Village in New York City, Shar in Detroit, and Walden House, Inc. in San Francisco. Instead of presenting an exhaustive list, we have chosen to delete items that are rare or have only historical interest. In addition, we have indicated, whenever possible, in which city (or area of the country) the term is most likely to be used.

Ace: LSD [NEW YORK]

Acid: LSD

Adam: MDMA

Alice B. Toklas: marijuana baked in a brownie

Amped: high on cocaine or speed

Andro: androstenedione (anabolic steroid used for body building)

Angel dust: PCP

Apache: fentanyl

Bacon: PMA

Banana split: LSD and 2C-B

Barbs: phenobarbital (barbiturate)

Base: freebase cocaine

Basuco: cocaine paste

Batman: PMA [NEW YORK]

BD: 1,4 butanediol (GHB precursor))

Belushi: speedball

Bennies: benzedrine (amphetamine)

Big K: ketamine [BROOKLYN, NY]

Bindle: small packet of drug

Black and White: speedball [NEW YORK]

Black beauties: Benzedrine (amphetamine)

Black tar: heroin

Blotter: LSD

Bomb: marijuana

Black: marijuana [NEW YORK]

Blow: cocaine (as in the movie of the same name)

Blue angels: amytal (barbiturate)

Blue moon: GHB

Blue nitro: GBL

Blunts: marijuana

Bolt: butyl nitrite

Bone: marijuana

Booger: cocaine [FLORIDA]

Boy: heroin [NEW YORK]

Breakfast cereal: ketamine [NEW YORK]

Bromo: 2CB

Brown: heroin

Bud: marijuana

Buddha (various spellings): marijuana

Bullet: paraphernalia used to measure an exact dose to be snorted

Bumble bees: PMA [NEW YORK]

Bummer: bad LSD trip

Bump: a short "line" (usually cocaine or methamphetamine)

Business man's special: DMT

Butter: cocaine [NEW YORK]

Buttons: peyote

Buzz kill: anything that brings you down when high

Candy flipping: a combination of MDMA and LSD

Cannabis: marijuana

Caps: psilocybin

Casper: MDMA [NEW YORK]

Cess: marijuana

Chasing the dragon: speedball (smoked) [NEW YORK]

Cheeba: marijuana

Cheese: heroin [SAN FRANCISCO]

Chemo: chemical octane booster

Chewy: marijuana and cocaine

Chiba: marijuana

Chicken crank: PMA

China: heroin [NEW YORK]

China pearl: heroin

China white: usually heroin (rarely fentanyl)

Chiva: brown heroin from Mexico

Chocolate: marijuana [NEW YORK]

Choke: marijuana

Christina: crystal meth

Chrissy: methamphetamine [NEW MEXICO]

Chronic: marijuana

Cid: LSD [NEW YORK]

Clarity: MDMA

Coke: cocaine

Cold turkey: sudden withdrawal from a drug

Crack: freebase cocaine

Crack on: get high on crystal meth [SAN FRANCISCO]

Crank: methamphetamine

Crash: sleep off exhaustion due to long drug run

Cream: cocaine

Cross tops: amphetamines

Cryllz: marijuana and freebase cocaine

Crystal meth: methamphetamine

Cubes: LSD [NEW YORK]

Dank: marijuana

Diesel: PCP [NEW YORK]

Dime bag: $10 worth of drug

Dips: PCP

Dirt: marijuana [NEW YORK]

Doja: marijuana

Doobie: marijuana cigarette

Dope: marijuana if smoked

Dope: heroin if "shot" (injected)

Doses: LSD

Dro: marijuana [NEW YORK]

Drop: Rohypnol

Dust: PCP

DXM: Dextromethorphan (ingredient in Robitussin)

E: MDMA

E-bombs: MDMA [NEW YORK]

Easy lay: GHB

Ecstasy: MDMA

Eight ball: 1/8th ounce of a drug

El: marijuana [NEW YORK]

Elaine: MDMA [NEW YORK]

Empathogen: a substance that facilitates empathy

Enliven: BD

Erica: MDMA

Euro dollars: PMA

Eve: MDEA

Evil one: crystal meth [NEW YORK]

Fire: marijuana [NEW YORK]

Fire water: once meant alcohol, now GBL

Fish scales: freebase cocaine

Flake: cocaine

Fluff: cocaine

Footballs: Xanax sticks [NEW YORK]

Forty (40): alcohol (malt liquor)

Four Twenty (420): marijuana

Freebase: crack cocaine

Fries: marijuana [KENTUCKY]

Fry: LSD [SAN FRANCISCO]

Fry: marijuana joints laced with embalming fluid and PCP [CONNECTICUT]

Fuel: PCP [NEW YORK]

G3: GBL

Ganja: marijuana [NEW YORK]

GBL: gamma butyl lactone (turns into GHB once ingested)

Georgia home boy: GHB

GHB: gamma hydroxybutyrate

Girl: cocaine [NEW YORK]

Glass: methamphetamine

Go: methamphetamine

Gofast: methamphetamine

Goofball (old): Doriden (barbiturate)

Goofball (new): heroin and cocaine [SAN FRANCISCO]

Grass: marijuana

Great bodily harm: GHB

Green: marijuana [BROOKLYN, NY]

Gyro: marijuana [NEW YORK]

Haze: marijuana [NEW YORK]

Herb: marijuana

Herbal ecstasy: ephedrine

Hillbilly heroin: OxyContin

Hippie flipping: LSD and psilocybin

Hits: LSD

Hog: PCP

Hop: heroin [BALTIMORE]

Horse: heroin

Hot rails: lines snorted with a heated glass straw [SAN FRANCISCO]

Housewives helper: Valium

Hubba: freebase cocaine

Hubs: freebase Cocaine

Huffing: inhaling volatile substance (glue or chemo) from a bag

Hydro: marijuana [NEW YORK]

Ice: smokable form of methamphetamine

Indica: marijuana

J: marijuana: [SAN FRANCISCO]

Jackpot: fentanyl

JIB: methamphetamine: [BRITISH COLUMBIA, CANADA]

John Belushi: speedball

Joint: marijuana cigarette

Jones (*noun*): a drug habit

Jones (*verb*): to crave

Junk: heroin

K: ketamine

K.B.: marijuana (kind bud)

K.G.B.: marijuana (killer green bud)

K-hole: ketamine induced disorientation

K.J.: PCP (krystal joint)

Katie: ketamine [NEW YORK]

Khat: cathinone

Kickin' it (old): detoxing from drug

Kickin' it (new): just hanging out

Kind: marijuana

L: marijuana [NEW YORK]

La Dama Blanca: cocaine

La Rocha: Rohypnol

Leaf: marijuana

Lick: ketamine [NEW YORK]

Line: finely chopped drug to be snorted

Liquid X: GHB

Locker room: butyl nitrite

Love drug: MDMA

Man: heroin [NEW YORK]

Mary Jane: marijuana

MDMA: methylenedioxymethamphetamine

Mesc: mescaline

Meth: methamphetamine

Mexican brown: heroin

Mickey Finn: chloral hydrate drops combined with alcohol

Molly: MDMA

Mushrooms: psilocybin

Negra: heroin

Nexus: 2CB

Nickel bag: $5 worth of any drug

Northern lights: marijuana [NEW YORK]

Nose candy: cocaine

Nuggets: marijuana [NEW YORK]

Number 3: codeine

O: opium

O.J.: opium joint (opium laced marijuana cigarette)

One-and-one: speedball [SAN FRANCISCO]

Oxy: OxyContin

Ozone: PCP

Pakalolo: marijuana [HAWAII]

Paper: LSD

Party pack: MDMA and 2C-B

PCP: phencyclidine

Pellets: Ritalin

Pink ladies: Darvon

PMA: paramethoxyamphetamine

Popcorn: cocaine [NEW YORK]

Poppers: amyl nitrite

Poppy: opium

Pot: marijuana

Pow-wow: heroin [SOUTH CAROLINA]

Powder: cocaine [NEW YORK]

Purple haze (old): LSD

Purple haze (new): marijuana [NEW YORK]

Quartz: smokable form of methamphetamine

Rail: a fat "line"

Rainbow flipping: MDMA and LSD and psilocybin [NEW YORK]

Rainbows: Tuinal (barbiturate)

Reds: Seconal (barbiturate)

Reefer: marijuana [NEW YORK]

Regs: marijuana

Rejoove: GBL

Renewtrient: GBL

Revivarant: GBL

Rib: Rohypnol

Roached out: high on Rohypnol

Roboing: Chugging cough syrup (Robitussin)

Rock: freebase cocaine

Rocky road: PCP and freebase cocaine

Roid rage: Anger associated with the use of steroids

Rolling: high on MDMA [SAN FRANCISCO]

Rope: marijuana

Ropies: Rohypnol

Ruffles: Rohypnol

Rush: butyl nitrite

Seven-up: cocaine

Shabs: methamphetamine [SAN FRANCISCO]

Shards: methamphetamine [SAN FRANCISCO]

Sherms: PCP laced cigarette [LOS ANGELES]

Shit: various drugs including: heroin, marijuana

Shrooms: magic mushrooms (psilocybin)

Sid: LSD

Sillycybin: psilocybin

Ski trips: cocaine

Skunk: marijuana

Sleepytime: heroin [NEW YORK]

Smack: heroin

Smoke: marijuana

Sniff: cocaine

Snow: cocaine

Solids: cocaine

Space base: freebase cocaine and PCP (smoked)

Special K: ketamine

Speed: methamphetamine

Speedball: heroin and cocaine combined

Spliff: marijuana [NEW YORK]

Sticks: marijuana [NEW YORK]

Sticky: marijuana

Stones: freebase cocaine [DETROIT]

Stuff: heroin

Tar: heroin

THC: tetrahydrocannabinol (the active ingredient in marijuana)

Tina: methamphetamine [NEW YORK]

TNT: fentanyl

Tom and Jerry: PMA

Toot: cocaine

Trail mix: combination of MDMA, ketamine, and methamphetamine

Trees: marijuana

Triple C: Coricidin (contains DMX) [WISCONSIN]

Tweek: methamphetamine

Tweaking: has taken too much speed and makes jerking movements

Twin turbo: PMA [NEW YORK]

2CB: psychedelic designer drug

2CT-2: psychedelic designer drug

2CT-7: psychedelic designer drug

Uzi: crack pipe

V: Valium (benzodiazepine)

Wake up: methamphetamine

Water: marijuana [NEW YORK]

Weed: marijuana

Wet: PCP

White: cocaine [SAN FRANCISCO]

White cheese: heroin

Whizz: freebase cocaine [NEW YORK]

Windowpane: LSD

X: MDMA

XTC: MDMA

Ya: cocaine

Yahoo: freebase cocaine

Yellow jackets: Nembutal (barbiturate)

Yeyo: cocaine [NEW YORK]

Zen: LSD (or sometimes GHB)

Zoom: methamphetamine

APPENDIX B

Resources

Books

The Eating Disorder Sourcebook: A Comprehensive Guide to the Causes, Treatments, and Prevention of Eating Disorders, by Carolyn Costin, McGraw-Hill, 1999.

A personal and professional viewpoint on eating disorders. Examines individual and family dynamics. Considers different solutions.

Overcoming Teen Depression: A Guide for Parents, by Miriam Kaufman, Firefly Books, 2001.

Explains what teen depression is and how to overcome it. Outlines current therapy and drug treatments. Thorough question and answer section for parents.

Buzzed: The Straight Facts About the Most Used and Abused Drugs from Alcohol to Ecstasy, by Cynthia Kuhn, Ph.D., Scott Swartzwelder, Ph.D., and Wilkie Wilson, Ph.D., W. W. Norton and Company, 1998.

An unbiased resource of information on legal and illegal drugs, and their effects on the brain and body.

Keys to Parenting Your Anxious Child, by Katharina Manassis, Barrons Educational Series, 1996.

Explains what anxiety is and is not, how it affects each family member, and how to cope with your anxious child. Information on medication and treatment.

When Your Child Has An Eating Disorder: A Step by Step Workbook for Parents and Other Caregivers by Abigail Nateshon, Jossey-Bass, 1999.
Information and concrete steps to take, treatment options, and tools to advocate for your child.

Helping Your Depressed Teenager: A Guide for Parents and Caregivers, by Gerald Oster and Sarah S. Montgomery, John Wiley and Sons, 1994.
A practical guide offering family solutions. Helps to distinguish between the subtle signs of depression and how to choose the right treatment options.

Give Your ADD Teen a Chance, by Lynn Weiss, Pinon Press, 1996.
Helps parents to determine which issues are caused by normal teenage development and which are caused by attention deficit disorder.

Toughlove, by Ted Wachtel and Phyllis and David York, Bantam Books, 1982.
This book covers the issues dealt with at the self-help program (with the same name) that deals with rebellious teenagers.

Teenagers with ADD: A Parent's Guide, by Chris A. Zeigler Dendy, Woodbine House, 1995.
A comprehensive look at the issues of attention deficit disorder, including diagnosis, treatment, family and school life, and interventions.

National Directory of Drug Abuse and Alcohol Treatment and Prevention Programs. Department of Health and Human Services. (800) 729-6686.

Organizations

All of these organizations have chapters around the country, and some even throughout the world (you can even find AA meetings on many cruise ships). You can look them up in your local telephone directory.

Alcoholics Anonymous (AA)
The original twelve-step recovery program, self-help for alcoholics.

Al-Anon and Alateen
A twelve-step recovery program for loved ones of an alcoholic. In Al-Anon, some groups focus on the issues of parents of using teens. Alateen is a separate group for teens with an alcoholic parent.

Co-Dependents Anonymous (CODA)
Another twelve-step recovery program, with a focus on life-long patterns of codependency.

Narcotics Anonymous (NA)
Based on the AA model, but with a focus on addicts of other drugs besides alcohol.

Nar-Anon
The twelve-step recovery program for loved ones of drug addicts.

Rational Recovery or SMART Recovery
A cognitive-behavioral approach to recovery.

Secular Organization for Sobriety (SOS.)
A self-help group with no religious or spiritual component. An answer for many who have been disappointed by AA.

TOUGHLOVE
An international organization for parents of rebellious teens.

Websites

http://www.dancesafe.org
A nonprofit, harm reduction organization, promoting health and safety within the rave and nightclub community. Information on raves, drug testing, guidelines for safe settings.

http://www.darnweb.com
The Drug and Alcohol Recovery Network is a drug and alcohol treatment center search engine. Find a treatment center near you by entering your zip code.

http://www.parentingteens.about.com
Information, insight, and support for parents of teens. Includes resources, education, a chat room.

http://www.samhsa.gov

The federal agency charged with improving the quality and availability of prevention and treatment services for substance abuse and mental illness. Lists all the agency's reports and services including a description of treatment centers around the nation.

http://www.toughlove.org

Nonprofit, self-help organization that provides ongoing education and active support to families, empowering parents and young people to accept responsibility for their actions.

http://www.teenchallenge.com

Information on drugs, treatment centers, and education programs.

The Twelve Steps of Alcoholics Anonymous

1. We admitted that we were powerless over alcohol, that our lives had become unmanageable.

2. We came to believe that a Power greater than ourselves could restore us to sanity.

3. We made a decision to turn our will and our lives over to the care of God *as we understood him.*

4. We made a searching and fearless moral inventory of ourselves.

5. We admitted to God, to ourselves, and to another human being the exact nature of our wrongs.

6. We were entirely ready to have God remove all these defects of character.

7. We humbly asked Him to remove our shortcomings.

8. We made a list of all persons we had harmed and became willing to make amends to them all.

9. We made direct amends to such people wherever possible, except when to do so would injure others.

10. We continued to take personal inventory and when we were wrong promptly admitted it.

11. We sought through prayer and meditation to improve our conscious contact with God, *as we understood Him*, praying only for knowledge of His will for us and the power to carry that out.

12. Having had a spiritual awakening as a result of these steps, we tried to carry this message to alcoholics and to practice these principles in all our affairs.

References

American Psychiatric Association (APA). 1994. *Diagnostic and Statistical Manual of Mental Disorders*. 4th ed. Washington, D.C.: American Psychiatric Press.

Anderson, C. M., et al. 2002. Abnormal T2 relaxation time in the cerebellar vermis of adults sexually abused in childhood: Potential role of the vermis in stress-enhanced risk for drug abuse. *Psychoneuroendocrinology* 27(1–2):231–244.

Beattie, M. 1996. *Codependent No More: How to Stop Controlling Others and Start Caring for Yourself*. 2nd ed. Center City, Minn.: Hazelden Publishing.

Centers for Disease Control and Prevention (CDC). 1998. Tobacco use among high school students—United States, 1997. *MMWR* 47:229-33.

Clark, D. B., L. Kirisci, and R. E. Tarter. 1998. Adolescent versus adult onset and the development of substance abuse disorders in males. *Drug and Alcohol Dependence* 49(2): 115–121.

DeWit, D. J., et al. 2000. The influence of early and frequent use of marijuana on the risk of desistance and of progression to marijuana-related harm. *Prevention Medicine* 31(5):455–464.

Foster, S., and L. Richter. 2002. *Teen Tipplers: America's Underage Drinking Epidemic*. New York: National Center on Addiction and Substance Abuse, Columbia University.

Gouzoulis-Mayfrank, E., et.al. 2000. Impaired cognitive performance in drug-free users of recreational ecstasy (MDMA). *Journal of Neurology, Neurosurgery, and Psychiatry* 68(6):719–725.

Grant, B. 1998. *The Impact of a Family History of Alcoholism on the Relationship between Age at Onset of Alcohol Use and DSM-IV Alcohol Dependence.* Bethesda, Md.: National Institute on Alcohol Abuse and Alcoholism, National Institute of Health.

Harlow, H. F., and R. Zimmerman. 1959. Affectional responses in the infant monkey. *Science* 130:421–432.

Heath, A. C. 1995. Genetic influences on alcoholism risk: A review of adoption and twin studies. *Alcohol Health and Research World: The Genetics of Alcoholism.* 19(3):166–171.

Hubbard, R. L., P. M. Flynn, S. G. Craddock, and B. W. Fletcher. 2001. Relapse after Drug Treatment. In *Relapse and Recovery in Addictions,* edited by F. M. Tims, C. G. Leukefeld, and J. J. Platt. New Haven, Conn.: Yale University Press.

Johnston, L. D., P. M. O'Malley, and J. G. Bachman. 2001. *Monitoring the Future National Results on Adolescent Drug Use: Overview of Key Findings, 2000.* (NIH Publication No. 01-4923). Bethesda, Md.: National Institute on Drug Abuse, National Institutes of Health.

Karpman, S. 1968. Fairy tales and script analysis. *Transactional Analysis Bulletin* 7(26):39–43.

Knight, J. R. 1997. Adolescent substance use: Screening, assessment, and intervention. *Contemporary Pediatrics* 14(4):45–72.

McKay, M., et al. 1996. *When Anger Hurts Your Kids.* Oakland, Calif.: New Harbinger Publications.

Nelson, D. D. 1978. *Frequently Seen Stages in Adolescent Chemical Use.* Minneapolis, Minn: CompCare Publications.

O'Neill, A., et al. 1998. Camp fear: David Van Blarigan's harrowing tale raises grave concerns about the secretive world of behavior-modification schools. *People,* August 3, 99–102.

Resnick, M. D., et al. 1997. Protecting adolescents from harm: Findings from the national longitudinal study of adolescent health. *Journal of the American Medical Association* 278(10):823–832.

Roper ASW (Audits and Surveys Worldwide, Inc., for Partnership for a Drug-Free America). 2001. Partnership Attitude Tracking Study (PATS).

SAMHSA (Substance Abuse and Mental Health Services Administration). 2001. *Summary of Findings from the 2000 National Household*

Survey on Drug Abuse. Rockville, Md.: U.S. Department of Health and Human Services: Substance Abuse and Mental Health Services Administration.

———. 1998. *Services Research Outcomes Study*. Rockville, Md.: U.S. Department of Health and Human Services: Substance Abuse and Mental Health Services Administration.

———. 1997. *National Treatment Improvement Evaluation Study*. Rockville, Md.: U.S. Department of Health and Human Services: Substance Abuse and Mental Health Services Administration.

Satir, V. 1988. *The New Peoplemaking*. Palo Alto, Calif.: Science and Behavior Books.

Schuckit, M. 1995. A long-term study of sons of alcoholics. *Alcohol Health and Research World: The Genetics of Alcoholism. National Institute on Alcohol Abuse and Alcoholism* 19(3):172–175.

Solowij, N., et al. 2002. The marijuana treatment project research group. *JAMA* 287:1123–1131.

Spitz, R. A. 1946. Anaclitic depression. *Psychoanalytic Study of the Child* 2:313–342.

Van Blarigan, D. 1998. Letter to the editor. *People*, August 24, 6.

Wall, T. L., and C. L. Ehlers. 1995. Genetic influences affecting alcohol use among Asians. *Alcohol Health and Research World: The Genetics of Alcoholism. National Institute on Alcohol Abuse and Alcoholism* 19(3):184–189.

Wegschieder-Cruse, S. 1989. *Another Chance: Hope and Health for the Alcoholic Family*. Palo Alto, Calif.: Science and Behavior Books.

Peter Rogers, Ph.D., is the Administrative Director of the Haight Ashbury Psychological Services. A retired psychotherapist, and former chief of the Chemical Dependency program at Kaiser Permanente, he is also the coauthor of three popular self-help books including *The Divorce Book, When Anger Hurts,* and *The Anger Control Workbook.* Peter lives in Northern California and enjoys traveling in Europe with his daughters.

Lea Goldstein, Ph.D., is a licensed psychologist with 17 years of experience working with teens and families struggling with drug and alcohol abuse and addiction. She has worked with Dual Diagnosed adolescents in an inpatient hospital, and before designed and implemented an outpatient program for teens and families at Kaiser in Oakland. The program included therapy groups for adolescents, a parent support group, a psychoeducational group for families, and a multi-family therapy group. She also maintains a private practice in which she sees adolescents and parents struggling with numerous developmental issues. Lea lives with her husband and teenage son in Northern California.

Some Other
New Harbinger Titles

The Daughter-In-Law's Survival Guide, Item DSG $12.95

Whose Life Is It Anyway?, Item $14.95

It Happened to Me, Item IHPM $17.95

Act it Out, Item AIO $19.95

Parenting Your Older Adopted Child, Item PYAO $16.95

Boy Talk, Item BTLK $14.95

Talking to Alzheimer's, Item TTA $12.95

Helping a Child with Nonverbal Learning Disorder or Asperger's Syndrome, Item HCNL $14.95

The 50 Best Ways to Simplify Your Life, Item FWSL $11.95

When Anger Hurts Your Relationship, Item WARY $13.95

The Couple's Survival Workbook, Item CPSU $18.95

Loving Your Teenage Daughter, Item LYTD $14.95

The Hidden Feeling of Motherhood, Item HFM $14.95

Parenting Well When Your Depressed, Item PWWY $17.95

Thinking Pregnant, Item TKPG $13.95

Pregnancy Stories, Item PS $14.95

The Co-Parenting Survival Guide, Item CPSG $14.95

Family Guide to Emotional Wellness, Item FGEW $24.95

How to Survive and Thrive in an Empty Nest, Item NEST $13.95

Children of the Self-Absorbed, Item CSAB $14.95

The Adoption Reunion Survival Guide, Item ARSG $13.95

Undefended Love, Item UNLO $13.95

Kid Cooperation, Item COOP $14.95

Call **toll free, 1-800-748-6273,** or log on to our online bookstore at **www.newharbinger.com** to order. Have your Visa or Mastercard number ready. Or send a check for the titles you want to New Harbinger Publications, Inc., 5674 Shattuck Ave., Oakland, CA 94609. Include $4.50 for the first book and 75¢ for each additional book, to cover shipping and handling. (California residents please include appropriate sales tax.) Allow two to five weeks for delivery.

Prices subject to change without notice.